T0056725

HERBAL TEA MAGIC

for the

MODERN WITCH

A Practical Guide to
**HEALING HERBS,
TEA LEAF READING, and
BOTANICAL SPELLS**

ELSIE WILD

Text copyright © 2021 Ellen Ricks. Design and concept copyright © 2021 Ulysses Press and its licensors. All rights reserved. Any unauthorized duplication in whole or in part or dissemination of this edition by any means (including but not limited to photocopying, electronic devices, digital versions, and the internet) will be prosecuted to the fullest extent of the law.

Published by:
ULYSSES PRESS
PO Box 3440
Berkeley, CA 94703
www.ulyssespress.com

ISBN: 978-1-64604-247-0
Library of Congress Control Number: 2021937735

Printed in the United States by Versa Press
10 9 8 7 6 5 4 3

Acquisitions editor: Ashten Evans
Managing editor: Claire Chun
Editor: Anne Healey
Proofreader: Barbara Schultz
Front cover design: Amy King
Interior design and layout: what!design @ whatweb.com
Artwork: shutterstock.com

NOTE TO READERS: This book has been written and published strictly for informational and educational purposes only. It is not intended to serve as medical advice or to be any form of medical treatment. You should always consult your physician before altering or changing any aspect of your medical treatment and/or undertaking a diet regimen, including the guidelines as described in this book. Do not stop or change any prescription medications without the guidance and advice of your physician. Any use of the information in this book is made on the reader's good judgment after consulting with his or her physician and is the reader's sole responsibility. This book is not intended to diagnose or treat any medical condition and is not a substitute for a physician.

This book is independently authored and published and no sponsorship or endorsement of this book by, and no affiliation with, any trademarked brands or other products mentioned within is claimed or suggested. All trademarks that appear in ingredient lists and elsewhere in this book belong to their respective owners and are used here for informational purposes only. The author and publisher encourage readers to patronize the quality brands mentioned in this book.

To Trixie,
Thanks for all the magic.

CONTENTS

AN INDUCTION INTO HERBAL TEA MAGIC

When most of us hear the word "witch," we tend to picture our favorites from movies and television: badass people with otherworldly powers, creating magic out of thin air with merely a snap of the finger or the recitation of some Latin phrase—something that could not be achieved off-screen.

Add in the term "witchcraft" or even "herbalism," and you may conjure up a different image: some old crone in a pointy hat stirring a giant black cauldron, dropping in strange ingredients, and working by candlelight. From an outsider's point of view, the craft may seem inaccessible, unattainable, and obsolete.

But all that is hocus-pocus.

Today, the modern witch mixes the magical with the mundane, giving older forms of witchcraft and divination a modern update. From drawing sigils on our cups of pumpkin spice latte to keeping a grimoire on our notes apps, modern witchcraft practices allow witches to tap into their magic in accessible ways. This is why herbalism and tasseography, or tea leaf divination, have become so valuable to today's witchcraft community. By using the knowledge that has been studied and practiced for centuries, we can brew our own magic.

Tasseography is one of the oldest forms of fortune-telling, allowing us to spill the tea on what the future holds for us. Our potions don't contain eyes of newt but rather rose petals and dandelion tea. Most of us have traded in foraging in the woods for creating herb gardens on our windowsills. We still carry the knowledge of herbalism within us—just with a new way of accessing it.

Herbal Tea Magic for the Modern Witch is precisely what the title states: an introductory guide to the magical world of herbal witchcraft: from learning about which plants you can add to your morning cup of tea, to crafting your own spells, to learning to read your destiny at the bottom of your cup. All while blending ancient knowledge, passed down from herbalists and witches for hundreds of years, with modern-day practices. No green thumb required.

My journey into herbal magic was a long one. I've never considered myself to be the "outdoorsy" type. I liked nature—if nature involved feeling the sun on my skin, walking barefoot in the grass, or being in or near a body of water. But actually being in nature: camping, hiking, or getting my heels caught in the mud? That was a hard pass for this witch. Despite being an earth sign (shout out to my fellow Virgo suns) and growing up right next to the Adirondack Mountains, the great outdoors never called to me. Even now, my green thumb still hasn't come in, evident by the several succulent plants I have recently killed. Cottagecore is a lovely aesthetic, but leave me in the woods to forage for food and I would be dead by sundown.

My introduction to the herbal magic world came during my junior year of college, sitting cross-legged in a metaphysical club meeting taking place in the supposedly haunted resident hall (yes, we were *that* kind of liberal arts college). During a tea reading party, I sipped cinnamon-flavored tea until I reached the bottom of my cup, amazed by what I saw there and by the fact that in decoding my leaves I had the freedom to follow my intuition rather than a set of firm rules like most divination practices. After the party, I brewed tea for everyone in my dorm to read their leaves. While I got plenty of eye rolls, my path to green witchcraft was set.

I spent the following years studying everything involving tea readings, including the different rituals to use. Soon, I began adding spells to the mix, and after some time, I began studying herbalism to learn what herbs, teas, and spices could aid my magic and life. I realized I didn't need to be "one with nature" to experience the wonders of herbalism; it was in the palm of my hand and at the bottom of my cup. Something as simple as a cup of tea suddenly became powerful in my hands.

This book is for the modern witch who follows their own magic, their own rules, and mother nature. For witches who are interested in creating their own potions, whether for healing, good fortune, or understanding their path. To love the earth in their own way and feel a connection to both the physical and the spiritual realms.

Oh, and to be a badass with a carryout cup in their hand.

In these pages, you will discover the meanings and uses of everyday herbs, how to cast spells, how to read tea leaves, and how to add other magical elements and drinks into your practice. But above all else, you will discover how to add a dash of magic to the mundane.

So, let's get started.

YOUR WITCH'S TOOL KIT

Just like with any craft, you are going to need the right set of tools and materials to make your potions, read your leaves, and cast your spells. However, you don't have to spend a lot of money on special "magical" tools like wands and spoons to get the best results. In fact, most of the things you'll need for this book you may already own or can get cheaply. Here's a basic list of materials you'll need to get started on your herbal magic journey.

GRIMOIRE: Because you'll be doing plenty of tea reading in this book, I encourage you to get a special notebook for your readings, spells, and even your own tea recipes—a herbal grimoire (book of spells), if you will. Not only will this keep all your information in one place, but it also will help you look back at past readings and spells and see how accurate they were and what their results were. Did your interpretations from a reading come to pass? What was the result of your money spell? Did you feel more confident after drinking a confidence tea? Keep a journal to keep track of everything—that's how you grow as a witch. For a modern witch twist, you can also keep a digital grimoire by putting all your readings, photos, and spells on your smart phone, on either your notes app or a particular journal app.

TEA INFUSER: As you can tell from the title of this book, we will be brewing a lot of tea, so you'll need a tea infuser to keep your blend together (unless you really like loose-leaf tea). Infusers come in many varieties, from stainless-steel mesh balls to fun animal shapes. You can also use reusable tea bags or teapots with built-in infusers.

 TEA AND HERBS: Yes, you are obviously going to need teas and herbs to make brews and do readings. See Chapter Two for a list of herbs you will need to get started (you may already have a few in your kitchen cupboard).

 STORAGE CONTAINERS FOR TEAS AND HERBS: Now that you have all your teas and herbs, you'll need someplace to put them. There are many ways to store your herbs, from the aesthetically pleasing, like glass vials or mason jars, to ziplock bags for convenience. The container that you end up using should be airtight so your herbs and spices don't go bad. If you're using clear containers, keep them in a dark, cool place so your herbs won't fade.

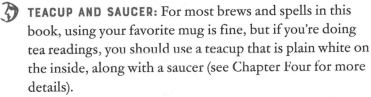 **TEACUP AND SAUCER:** For most brews and spells in this book, using your favorite mug is fine, but if you're doing tea readings, you should use a teacup that is plain white on the inside, along with a saucer (see Chapter Four for more details).

SPOON: A simple kitchen tool, the spoon will act as a wand for most of your herbal blends and spells. You can use any old spoon in your kitchen, or you can get witchy and buy a fancy spoon with a crystal at the end of the handle, usually found any place witchy supplies are sold.

MORTAR AND PESTLE: For an old-school witch vibe, use a mortar and pestle to grind up your herbs and spices to blend them in your tea.

INTERNET ACCESS: For a modern witch, technology is essential, as it offers you an almost unlimited amount of knowledge to help you make the best potions and spells. Plus, it's also easy to keep track of your success through journal apps.

 YOUR OWN MAGIC: Found within you (yes, cringe, I know).

Medical Warnings: Because this book will be working with a variety of different plants that you will be consuming, it's vital to consult a doctor and a certified herbalist before trying any recipe in this book or making your own herbal blend if you have any medical condition, especially if you have any bleeding disorders or allergies, or are taking any medication. If you are pregnant or nursing, hold off on trying out the teas and herbal blends in the book until you're finished. And remember, Google is a witch's best friend, so Google any plants before you eat them—especially if you found them out in the wild. Collecting herbs is cute in cartoon movies but not cute if you accidentally eat nightshade and die.

Chapter 1

THE HISTORY OF HERBALISM AND TASSEOGRAPHY

*B*efore we can dive into herbal magic, tea reading, and other magical fun, we must first understand what herbal magic is, because if we don't understand it, we won't be able to appreciate it or use it to its full potential. So, what is herbal magic? How do we know what herbs heal an upset stomach and what herbs make us sick? What herbs bring prosperity, and what ones bring danger? This knowledge has been developed for thousands of years using herbalism.

Herbalism is the folk practice of studying and using plants for their healing benefits. Witches may also use knowledge gained from herbalism to study, understand, and use plants for their magical properties. When we use the term "herb," we are talking about every part of the plant, from the root to the petals. However, some parts of the plant have different medical and magical properties from other parts.

Not all herbalists consider themselves to be witches, just as not all witches use plants and herbs in their craft. However, witches tend to put the information gained from herbalism to use in their craft. Early herbalists came from all types of backgrounds, from medical scholars to cunning folk who lived on the outskirts of town, each providing healing to those who need it.

HISTORY OF HERBALISM

Herbalism has been practiced throughout the world, dating back to the prehistoric era. One of the earliest known writings of herbalism, a list of healing plants, was written by the Sumerians in ancient Mesopotamia. Similar writings have been found from ancient Egypt and ancient Greece. Every region in the world has its own unique herbs, remedies, and cultural practices. One form of herbalism that is still practiced today is Traditional Chinese Medicine, also known as TCM, which uses various techniques, from acupuncture to herbal remedies, to address and cure health problems. Another is Ayurveda, a holistic medicine practice from India that has been used for 5,000 years and often incorporates herbalism. However, while TCM and Ayurveda have been preserved because of written documentation of their practice, most herbalism was passed down orally from practitioner to student.

For many years, this oral tradition worked because people used to live in small villages where there would be only one person who practiced herbalism and folk magic. This person, usually (but not always) a woman, would go by many names: healer, midwife, shaman, herbalist, medicine man/woman, or wise man/woman. It would be this person who grew the needed herbs for the community, and who community members would turn to for healing, both physical (e.g., headaches, fevers, stomach aches, childbirth, illness) and emotional and spiritual (e.g., heartbreak, love spells, luck, prosperity, relieving grief). The healer knew that each plant was sacred, holding its own essence of magic, and they knew how to use it to help others.

However, things changed during the rise of a deadly combination of Christianity and colonialism that suppressed and nearly erased herbalism from this world. Folk healing was branded as "witchcraft" and "the dark arts." The midwives who had been an important part of the community were burned at the stake throughout Europe. In Africa, people were ripped from their homes and their medicines and sold into slavery overseas. India nearly lost its healing practices due to centuries of being invaded by different colonialists seeking to erase all hints of their culture. Whoever wasn't killed was driven underground, forced to hide their knowledge.

But the people fought back. The Irish fought tirelessly to protect their herbs and plant life from multiple invasions. Africans who were forced onto ships smuggled in the seeds of plants with significant spiritual and medicinal value, even it meant risking their very lives, and planted them in a new world. These people knew that they were fighting, and even dying, for something important.

And the magic lived on.

Though most people are quick to call herbalism "nonsense" and "quackery," you can still see the magic live on in small ways, even if you come from a very unmagical and non-spiritual background. You get sick with a sore throat and your grandmother makes you bone broth with turmeric. You send your best friend yellow roses because you heard it symbolizes friendship and caring. You drink chamomile tea before bed to help you fall asleep. You plant a rosemary bush in your front yard because one of your "interesting" aunts told you it would protect your house. In all these small ways, you are practicing herbal magic.

Even today, when herbalism has become mainstream, it's still not treated with the respect and care it deserves. Many medical professionals still roll their eyes at homemade healing balms and teas, and certain "wellness" brands make a profit off of cultural appropriation by overharvesting sacred plants like white sage, exploiting colonized people who rely on and treasure those plants.

However, there are many ways to ethically use herbal magic, and the power found in these plants can be used in balms, salves, poppets (a doll, sometimes filled with herbs and crystals, made for casting spells on a certain person), bath soaks, and teas.

THE "TEA" ON TEA

Obviously, in a book about herbal magic and tasseography, we will be doing an awful lot of tea talk. While you may have enjoyed tea often, maybe even calling yourself a tea snob, how much do you really know about your favorite brew?

Almost all teas we enjoy and consume today (black, green, oolong, and white) come from one plant species, *Camellia sinensis*, sometimes referred to as the "tea plant." The *Camellia sinensis* plant is an evergreen forest shrub with glossy green leaves. These leaves are similar to the bay leaf as they are both the same shape and have similar serrated edges. The *Camellia sinensis* originated in the southwest region of China, in Yunnan Province.

SPILLING THE TEA: Despite its common usage in marketing and in our own descriptions, there is no such thing as "herbal tea." No, your brew of peppermint leaves is not peppermint tea. Same with the lavender petals you brew with some lemon balm. That's because to make tea, you need leaves that come from the *Camellia sinensis* plant, either the *Camellia sinensis sinensis* (Chinese tea) variety or the *Camellia sinensis assamica* (Indian tea) variety. If it doesn't come from the *Camellia sinensis*, it's not tea; it's just an herbal blend or brew. But I guess that would be wordy to put on a tea box.

The origins of tea drinking are unclear. The popular myth about how tea come to be is that in 2737 BC, Emperor Shennong was sitting under a tea tree with his pot of boiled water. The leaves of the tea plant fell into his bowl and turned the water a golden color. The emperor, sort of a scientist, was overcome by curiosity and took a sip. Amazed at the flavor, he began to research the plant and discovered the leaves' medicinal properties and delicious flavors.

While that's a great story, there's not much evidence to back it up. One of the earliest written texts on tea drinking was found in a medical text written by a Chinese physician, Hua Tuo, around the third century AD, though it is believed that tea was used for healing purposes long before it was written down. Originally, tea was often used to treat digestive issues. Even today, the Chinese prefer to drink tea after meals to aid digestion.

However, while tea was drunk by members of Chinese royalty or used solely as medicine, tea really became a popular drink during the Tang dynasty (618–906 AD). People would perform elaborate tea rituals to drink their brews. Buddhist monks really enjoyed tea because it kept them awake during long meditation periods.

The magic of tea stayed in China until the late eighth century, when two important things happened. Tea master Lu Yu wrote the world's first book about tea, *Cha Jing*, or *The Classic of Tea*, which helped define Chinese tea culture. Also, Japanese monks visited China during this time and studied the *Camellia sinensis* plant, taking samples back home with them. This became the start of Japanese tea culture.

While China traded tea to Tibet, the Turks, Arab countries, and India, tea did not reach Europe until the late seventeenth century, when Dutch traders imported it to Holland. Soon tea became a popular drink in Holland, and the trend quickly spread throughout Western Europe. Tea was only consumed by the very rich until the tea trade made the drink affordable to everyone who wanted it. However, that trade came at a high moral cost, steeped in colonialism, violence, slavery, and revolution.

Today, tea is still one of the most popular drinks globally. While many still consume it for pleasure, many drink it for its health benefits and magical benefits.

TASSEOGRAPHY

Tasseography, also known as tasseomancy, is one of the oldest forms of divination. But although tea originated in China, it's difficult for historians to pinpoint where exactly tasseomancy originated. Tasse comes from the Arabic word for "cup," while -mancy is the Greek suffix for "divination"; so the word "tasseomancy" can literally be translated as "divining from the cup." However, most Middle Eastern and Greek diviners did not use tea when performing their cup reading. Instead, they used thick coffee, where the heavy grounds settled on the bottom of their cups.

The tasseography that we know today began during Britain's Victorian Age when members of the upper class developed a fascination with the occult, including fortune-telling. Wealthy society women hired Romani fortune-tellers to read their teacup and reveal their fortunes. It made sense for tea to be used in these readings because of its popularity and the fact that tea was drunk loose, since tea bags were not invented until 1903. The leaves would settle to the bottom anyway, making it easy to see the symbols below. While most people who practiced tasscography were Romani, the first book about tea leaf reading published in English during the eighteenth century was written by a Highland seer.

Today, the practice of tasseography continues to live on all over the world, especially in England, Ireland, and Scotland. With modern witchcraft, green witchery, and herbal magic, witches are adding their own magical touch as they continue to learn about herbs and are putting their own spin on tea readings.

But what is the significance of these herbs? What magic lies in tea leaves and coffee grounds anyway? And where do we find these magical properties?

You're about to find out.

Chapter 2

AN INTRODUCTION TO TEAS AND HERBS

*B*efore we get into potions, spells, and all that witch stuff, it's important to learn more about the herbs and teas we will be using throughout the book. These are our tools, and they must be handled with care, especially when we are working with herbs that could affect our bodies in not-so-magical ways, so pay extra attention to medical warnings. This list includes the most common and most popular teas and herbs used in the tea world. Many of these can be found in your grocery store, farmers' market, or local witch shop if you are lucky enough to be near one. Some herbs, such as peppermint, lavender, and rose, can be grown at home, while others, like rooibos, may be harder (and more expensive) to get your hands on but are very popular. This list is mainly to expand your botanical horizons and to encourage you to play around as you become comfortable with brewing and crafting potions.

TEAS

While there are hundreds of different kinds of tea in the world, there are four main types of tea: black, green, oolong, and white.

BLACK TEA

One of the most versatile teas, black tea is a more oxidized version of green tea, with a stronger flavor and more caffeine (though much less than a cup of coffee). Because of its full flavor, black tea acts as a great base for most tea blends and potions. Black tea originated in China in the seventeenth century when the Chinese started fermenting tea leaves to extend their storage life. Black tea came to Europe in the eighteenth century, charming the British aristocracy and eventually all of England. Black tea is the main ingredient in classic tea blends such as English breakfast tea and Earl Grey tea.

Magical Properties: Strength, stability, endings, finished business, banishment, expelling negativity, energy boost, courage, mental clarity, grounding, cleansing. Associated with the earth element and winter.

Health Properties: Boosts metabolism, boosts immunity, relieves stress, improves bone health, eases asthma, kills bacteria, lowers cholesterol, lowers risk of diabetes, increases energy, decreases digestive activity.

Medical Warnings: Pregnant people should not drink more than two cups of black tea a day.

Different Types: English breakfast, Earl Grey, chai, Assam, Darjeeling.

Brewing Tip: For the best taste, brew black tea in about 180°F–210°F water and let it steep for four to eight minutes, depending on the blend.

GREEN TEA

A staple for any tea lover, green tea is made from the unoxidized leaves of the *Camellia sinensis* plant. It's called green tea because the leaves are harvested when they are slightly withered and immediately cooked before they oxidize, thus keeping their green coloring. *Camellia sinensis* leaves for green tea are harvested three times a year to get the highest quality. Green tea was initially used for medical purposes to treat a range of illnesses. For many decades, green tea was symbol of status and wealth due to its cost and lengthy preparation. But today green tea can be enjoyed by anyone. Matcha, green tea's popular cousin, in made from the ground powder of shade-grown green tea leaves, which is whisked together with hot water in a ceramic bowl. Matcha was originally used in traditional Japanese tea ceremonies but is now popular everywhere.

Magical Properties: Healing, love, mindfulness, passion, cleansing, regulating energy, wealth. Associated with the fire element and spring.

Health Properties: Boosts metabolism, improves brain function, supports sexual health, supports heart health, rich in antioxidants. Could also increase longevity.

Medical Warnings: None.

Different Types: Chunmee green tea, gunpowder green tea, jasmine green tea, and matcha.

Brewing Tip: Green tea tastes best when brewed at a mild water temperature (about 180°F) and steeped for about three minutes. Water that is too hot could make the tea bitter.

OOLONG TEA

While black, green, and white tea are easily recognizable to most people, oolong tends to throw people off. Sure, you've heard of it, but what is it? Oolong is a semi-oxidized tea made from the leaves of the *Camellia sinensis* plant. The amount of time the tea is oxidized varies, which makes each oolong flavor unique. Oolong tea gets its name from two Chinese words meaning "black dragon," a reference to the way the leaves are rolled into curly shapes resembling dragons.

Magical Properties: Wisdom, beauty, emotional balance and connection, romance, friendship, serenity, divination, reflection. Associated with the water element and autumn.

Health Properties: Lowers blood pressure, improves sleep, improves gut health, supports heart health, boosts metabolism, improves brain health, increases bone density, prevents tooth decay. Increases alertness and improves your mood.

Medical Warnings: None.

Brewing Tip: Oolong tastes best when it's brewed at a water temperature of 185°F–206°F and steeped for around four minutes. Oolong tea actually tastes better the more you re-steep it.

WHITE TEA

A highly delicate tea made from the unopened buds of the *Camellia sinensis* plant, white tea is produced with minimal processing during a short harvesting season, creating its unique floral flavor and its expensive price tag. White tea, which originated in the Fujian Province of China during the sixteenth century, has become popular for its taste, health benefits, and magical powers.

Magical Properties: Purification, protection, clarity, realization, meditation, cleansing, psychic abilities, youth, blessings, new beginnings, happiness, wisdom. Associated with the air element, summer, and moon magic.

Health Properties: Reduces the risk of heart disease, lowers insulin resistance, protects against osteoporosis, helps skin damage, reduces the risk of cancer, rich in antioxidants.

Medical Warnings: None.

Different Types: Silver Needle (BaiHao YinZhen), White Peony (Bai Mu Dan), Tribute Eyebrow (Gong Mei), Long Life Eyebrow (Shou Mei).

Brewing Tip: Because of its delicate nature, white tea should be made with 175°–185°F water and steeped for one to three minutes maximum or it will turn bitter.

HERBS AND SPICES

Here is your starter guide to the common herbs and spices that all witches should have in their cabinet, or should at least be aware of. This is not a definitive list but more of an introduction to help you begin learning about and using your herbs and spices to the best of your abilities. Remember, these are your tools; take good care of them.

BLACKBERRY LEAF

Blackberries, the fruit, have a long history in witchcraft, mostly associated with European pagans. According to Celtic lore, blackberries were the fruit of the fae (fairies) and was unlucky to eat. However, many used blackberries to cure illnesses and in rituals. Just as blackberries were magical, their leaves also contain their own magical and healing properties as well.

What It Looks Like: Found on top of a blackberry, these leaves are typically light green in color, with each leaf consisting of three to five oval leaflets.

Flavor Profile: Fruity.

Magical Properties: Healing, money, protection.

Health Properties: Eases sore throats, heals mouth sores and ulcers, rich in antioxidants.

Medical Warnings: Do not consume if you have any type of liver disease.

CALENDULA

Calendula, also known as pot marigold, is a bright, cheerful little flower with a mild taste, but it packs a magical punch. Known as the sun herb, calendula is one of the oldest known herbs in herbalism. It was used throughout ancient Greece, Egypt, India, and Arabia for various purposes, from making the skin look renewed to serving as an antidote to poisoning. During the American Civil War, doctors carried dried calendula petals in their pockets to stop the bleeding of war wounds. On the magical side of things, calendula was used in love potions, its petals were scattered under beds for protection, and upset lovers would wear a garland of the plant to show their jealousy.

What It Looks Like: Pot marigolds are tall plants with bright orange petals that are straight and long, similar to daisies. The flower is used in teas, often dried first.

Flavor Profile: Slightly bitter but earthy and floral.

Magical Properties: Protection (especially in legal matters), spiritual powers, wealth, healing, stability, dreamwork, love, marriage.

Health Properties: Nourishes skin, hair, and nails; rich in antioxidants; relieves sore throats; regulates the menstrual cycle; relieves sore muscles; anti-inflammatory.

Medical Warnings: Do not use if you have an allergy to other plants in the Asteraceae family (such as chamomile), are pregnant, or are on blood-pressure medication.

CARDAMOM

If you want to spice up your regular tea, look no further than cardamom, the magical spice that is both sweet and savory. A regular feature in Indian, Middle Eastern Arabic, and Swedish cuisine, it's also used in various beverages, such as Turkish coffee and masala chai, a black tea drink made with milk, sugar, cardamom, black pepper, ginger, and various other spices. Cardamom is native to India and was brought to Western culture by the ancient Macedonian king Alexander the Great in the fourth century BC.

What It Looks Like: Cardamom comes from a flowering plant in the ginger family. It is made from the plant's spindle-shaped seed pod. The color of the pod is either green (green cardamom or true cardamom) or black (black cardamom), while the seeds inside are small and black. You can use the pods whole or grind them up.

Flavor Profile: Strong, sweet, with a hint of lemon and mint. Black cardamom has a smoky note to it.

Magical Properties: Clarity, courage, direction, wisdom, love, lust.

Health Properties: Lowers blood pressure, rich in antioxidants, relieves nausea and other digestive issues, prevents cavities, treats infections, treats bad breath, improves breathing, lowers blood sugar, reduces anxiety, protects the liver.

Medical Warnings: None.

CHAMOMILE

One of the most popular ingredients to add to tea, chamomile has been used in nighttime teas for ages as it's the perfect relaxer. Chamomile tea is made from the flowers of dried chamomile and has been used as medicine for centuries.

What It Looks Like: With its white petals and cone-shaped yellow center, chamomile looks similar to a daisy but is much smaller.

Flavor Profile: Sweet, floral.

Magical Properties: Love, banishment, purification, calming, prosperity, healing, peace.

Health Properties: Reduces anxiety, reduces menstrual pain, lowers blood sugar, reduces inflammation, prevents osteoporosis, treats cold symptoms.

Medical Warnings: Avoid using chamomile if you have severe ragweed allergies or are allergic to chamomile or chamomile products. Keep away from young children.

CINNAMON

Always a crowd pleaser, cinnamon is a spice-cabinet staple and a much-loved ingredient in many desserts. Witches love cinnamon for its magical benefits and its versatility; you can put it in almost anything—teas, coffees, hot chocolate, ciders—and it will both taste delicious and be magical. You can even use it in candle making for its wonderful smell. Kitchen witches love to use this spice in their baking spells as well. Cinnamon is often a key ingredient in chai.

What It Looks Like: Most of the time, cinnamon is already ground into a fine brown powder, but you can also buy cinnamon sticks, which are long and brown sticks, and look like tree bark.

Flavor Profile: Sweet, woody, with a spicy kick.

Magical Properties: Luck, success, energy, happiness, creativity, money, psychic boost, healing, protection, love magic, communicating with the spirit. Also associated with the sun and fire.

Health Properties: Reduces blood sugar, treats chronic wounds, heart health, treats digestive issues, improves memory, lowers blood pressure.

Medical Warnings: It's important not to consume more than one teaspoon of cinnamon a day because large doses of cinnamon can have negative side effects. If you are on diabetes medication, talk to your doctor about how much cinnamon is safe for you.

CLOVES

A key ingredient in gingerbread, pumpkin pie, and Indian cuisine, cloves are a versatile spice that adds warm flavor. Originating in Indonesia, cloves have been used in Chinese medicine and Ayurvedic medicine for years. Witches love cloves, especially during the spooky season, as it's a popular ingredient in pumpkin spice.

What It Looks Like: Whole cloves are small, reddish-brown, and shaped like small spikes. Cloves can be used whole or ground up.

Flavor Profile: Subtle sweet flavor full of warmth.

Magical Properties: Protection, banishing negativity, love, money.

Health Properties: Rich in antioxidants, promotes healthy liver function, cases toothaches, treats sinus infections, aids digestion, reduces fever.

Medical Warnings: Ask your doctor before consuming cloves if you have a bleeding or blood-clotting disorder or are about to have surgery.

CORNFLOWER

The patron herb of herbalists, cornflower is a beautiful flower to add to any tea for both its potent magical abilities and the aesthetic appeal of its vibrant blue petals, worthy of any Instagram picture. Another name for cornflower is bachelor's button because young men used to wear the flower on their lapel to let people know they were single and ready to go courting.

What It Looks Like: You can easily identify cornflower by the bright blue color of its papery petals. The flower heads are surrounded by bracts, giving them their full shape. They also attract butterflies.

Flavor Profile: Slightly spicy with a touch of sweetness.

Magical Properties: Protection, love, fertility, sex, psychic abilities, abundance, self-knowledge, spirituality, growth, creativity.

Health Properties: Lowers fevers, decreases bloating, relieves chest congestion, helps with weak eyes.

Medical Warnings: Avoid if you are pregnant, are breastfeeding, or have allergies to ragweed or daisies.

DANDELION

Long the villain to many lawn care fanatics, dandelions have gotten a bad rap by being labeled a "weed." However, every part of this lovely yellow flower has been used in herbalism for centuries, with the root being especially prized for its healing and magical properties. So put away your weed killer and start saving your dandelions.

What It Looks Like: While the dandelion has a bright yellow head, its root is found deep in the earth and is shaped like a long, white carrot. The root can be cut up, dried, or ground into a powder. The leaves can also be dried and used in teas.

Flavor Profile: Toasty and nutty.

Magical Properties: Divination, wish-granting, good luck, psychic powers, dream magic, spirit work, cleansing, air magic.

Health Properties: Can be used as a diuretic, reduces inflammation, reduces cholesterol, lowers blood pressure, reduces constipation, boosts the immune system.

Medical Warnings: Do not take if you have a weed allergy, are pregnant or nursing, or are taking antidepressants, diuretics, estrogen-based contraceptives, or antibiotics.

ELDERFLOWER

A common magical ingredient found in many teas, potions, and brews, this enchanted flower comes from the sacred elder tree. The elder tree is often associated with the winter solstice, which is the transition from the dark to the light and a time of rebirth. This is fitting since elder can grow anew from dead wood. It is also associated with fairies because many Northern European folk traditions consider the elder to be from the fairy land. Elderflower has its own magical and healing benefits as well.

What It Looks Like: Elderflowers are tiny white flowers grown in sprays (or groups) on elder trees. These flowers are dried and used in teas.

Flavor Profile: Sweet floral flavor.

Magical Properties: Protection, rebirth, prosperity, endings, psychic awareness, grounding, joy, emotional healing and calming, rest, connection with fairies.

Health Properties: Treats sinus infections, boosts the immune system, fights off colds and flus, rich in vitamin C, mild diuretic.

Medical Warnings: Uncooked or undried elderflower could cause nausea, vomiting, and diarrhea. Do not consume in large amounts.

While the dried flower petals are safe, stay away from the leaves and roots of the elder tree. Do not use when pregnant.

FENNEL SEEDS

Originally native to the Mediterranean, fennel, a hardy herb that is a member of the carrot family, is now used globally in savory dishes, medicines, and witchcraft. It has a wide range of applications, from treating stomach irritation to protecting the home from negative energies. In fact, many witches use fennel as an alternative to sage for cleansing. For teas, fennel seeds work best rather than the actual fennel plant or stalk.

What It Looks Like: Fennel seeds are light-green, oval-shaped seeds with ridges. When dried, they take on a greenish-brown color.

Flavor Profile: Similar to licorice, with a slightly bitter aftertaste. Very aromatic.

Magical Properties: Courage, strength, protection, fertility, love, healing, divination, longevity, cleansing.

Health Properties: Fights colds, relaxes the muscles, aids sleep, increases milk production, helps an upset stomach, full of antioxidants, relieves constipation.

Medical Warnings: Do not take if you are pregnant; allergic to carrots, celery, or mugwort; if you are taking blood thinners; or if you have a bleeding disorder.

GINGER

One of the world's oldest recognized medical plants, ginger is a flowering plant native to Southeast Asia. It was first mentioned in

Chinese writing in 400 BC. Today, India is the highest producer of ginger. The part of the plant that is used is called "ginger root," although it is not actually a root but a rhizome, or modified underground stem. This herb is a common item in most people's kitchens, whether it's fresh or kept as a dried powder in the spice cabinet.

What It Looks Like: Ginger's rhizome is a light brown color on the outside and a light yellow on the inside. It has several gnarly branches or "fingers," making it easy to recognize.

Flavor Profile: Sweet but slightly peppery, giving it some spice.

Magical Properties: Confidence, clarity, sensuality, quick manifestation, increased energy and personal power, healing, retribution, money, passion, balance, success.

Health Properties: Helps with nausea, eases arthritis pain, lowers cholesterol, anti-inflammatory, antiviral.

Medical Warnings: Talk to your doctor about taking ginger if you have a heart condition, diabetes, and/or gallstones.

GINSENG

Thanks to popular mainstream "wellness" brands, it's hard to find any products, from smoothies to herbal blends, that don't have some ginseng in them. However, before its mainstream fame, ginseng had been a treasured medicine in Traditional Chinese Medicine for centuries, providing energy and healing. It also has been used in magic for similar purposes. There are eleven types of ginseng, including Asian ginseng, American ginseng, white ginseng, and Korean red ginseng. So, look closely before picking one up.

What It Looks Like: Ginseng is a light-colored, forked-shaped root that grows in the ground; above ground, the ginseng plant has long stalks topped with green, oval-shaped leaves. It takes a very long time for the plant to grow, which can make the spice rare. For example, fresh ginseng means it's been harvested before the plant has turned four. White ginseng is usually harvested when the plant is about four to six years old, and red ginseng is harvested after six or more years. Ginseng root can be used fresh, dried, or ground.

Flavor Profile: Earthy, bitter, with just a hint of sweetness.

Magical Properties: Love, lust, beauty, wealth, vitality, protection, wishes, spirituality.

Health Properties: Boosts mood, improves memory, boosts the immune system, fights fatigue, promotes energy, boosts sex drive.

Medical Warnings: May reduce the effectiveness of anticoagulant drugs.

HIBISCUS

This tropical flower is more than just beautiful to look at; it also contains magical and healing properties when added to your tea. Whether you drink it hot or cold, hibiscus adds a magic touch to your day.

What It Looks Like: Hibiscus flowers are large, trumpet-shaped flowers that grow on dark-green shrubs. While the fresh petals are bright red, when dried they turn a pink to dark-red color.

Flavor Profile: Tart, cranberry-like.

Magical Properties: Divination, love, lust, peace, passion.

Health Properties: Improves liver health, fights bacterial infections, lowers blood pressure, helps with menstrual cramps, helps with depression, aids with digestive issues.

Medical Warnings: Can cause hypotension or hypoglycemia if taken with diabetes or blood-pressure medication.

LAVENDER

A spa-day essential—who doesn't love lavender? It's a beautiful flower with a soothing aroma, and it's a dream to work with for both herbalists and witches alike. Lavender has become very trendy in recent years, used in everything from teas to desserts. Still, this lovely herb has been around for over 2,500 years. It is native to the Mediterranean, India, and the Middle East, but you can grow lavender almost anywhere.

What It Looks Like: Lavender has grey-green leaves and whorls of tiny deep-bluish-purple flowers held on spikes rising above the leaves.

Flavor Profile: Sweet and earthy.

Magical Properties: Happiness, healing, love, protection, wealth, relaxation, sleep, dream magic.

Health Properties: Decreases anxiety; helps with insomnia, depression, and headaches; decreases nausea and pain after surgery. It could also help with acne issues and skin irritation.

Medical Warnings: Do not take with another sedative.

LEMON BALM

The delight of herbalists, witches, and tea fans alike, lemon balm is a very popular herb that brings tangy, uplifting energy just from its aroma alone. Lemon balm is also known as Melissa, which is Greek for "honeybee." In ancient Turkey, lemon balm was planted near beehives to encourage the bees to return home. Lemon balm is a favorite of herbalists for its many health benefits. In fact, in medieval Europe, lemon balm tea was known as "the elixir of youth." While the herb is native to Europe, North Africa, and West Africa, it can be grown all over the world.

What It Looks Like: A leafy green plant with heart-shaped leaves that grow opposite each other on a square stem.

Flavor Profile: Lemony, citrus taste.

Magical Properties: Love, success, healing, friendship, attraction (especially attraction to a romantic partner or friends), spiritual development.

Health Properties: Heals colds, flu, fevers, sore throats, cold sores, and other viruses; relieves stress; reduces anxiety; promotes calmness; boosts cognitive function; eases insomnia; relieves indigestion; treats nausea. It can also minimize menstrual cramps, headache pains, and toothaches—basically, a balm for all things.

Medical Warnings: Talk to your doctor before taking lemon balm if you are on glaucoma or thyroid medication. Do not take if you are taking a sedative, are on antidepressants, or are pregnant.

WHAT KIND OF LEMON HERB TO USE?

Because lemon is a popular flavor in tea, it may be difficult for new witches and tea drinkers to decide between three similar-sounding herbs: lemon balm, lemongrass, and lemon verbena. While these three are remarkably similar, there are a few key reasons why lemongrass and lemon verbena are different from lemon balm. Lemon balm has a stronger lemon flavor than both lemongrass and lemon verbena; lemongrass is more astringent. Lemongrass also looks like grass rather than a shrub or some leaves. They also have different magical and health properties.

LEMONGRASS

A common staple of spas and lotions, lemongrass is commonly used in skin care products because of their calming, lemony scent that isn't overpowering. Lemongrass is a great option for those who want the magic of lemon but a milder taste.

What It Looks Like: Lemongrass is, well grass. In the wild, lemongrass looks like regular grass, only when its cut does lemongrass look similar to green onions with its pale, yellow-green stalk, though it has a citrus scent to it.

Flavor Profile: Milder lemon taste than lemon balm.

Magical Properties: Protection, increased psychic ability, cleansing, healing, growth, lust.

Health Properties: The same as lemon balm, especially for relieving anxiety, indigestion, and bloating; also rich in antioxidants.

Medical Warnings: Lemongrass should not be consumed if you are pregnant or have low potassium levels.

LEMON VERBENA

While not as well-known as lemon balm and lemongrass, lemon verbena is famous in its own right for its powerful lemon flavor, making it a great addition in any teas where you want an extra burst of flavor.

What It Looks Like: A yellow-green plant with pointed leaves, usually used dried in teas.

Flavor Profile: Stronger lemon flavor than lemon balm.

Magical Properties: Purification, love, protection from nightmares, strength, creativity.

Health Properties: Same as lemon balm and lemongrass.

Medical Warnings: Lemon verbena should not be used if you are pregnant, and it can make kidney disease worse.

LICORICE ROOT

One of the world's oldest herbal remedies, licorice may not be a popular candy flavor, but it's certainly a favorite herb for both witches and herbalists. The licorice plant is native to Western Asia and Southern Europe, and the use of licorice root dates back as far as ancient Egypt, where the root was made into sweet healing drinks for pharaohs. Fun fact: licorice candies are not actually flavored with licorice root. They are flavored with essential oil from anise, which has a similar taste. The more you know!

What It Looks Like: The root of the licorice plant looks similar to twigs: long, thin, and light brown. It is ground up when added to tea.

Flavor Profile: A cross between bitterness and sweetness.

Magical Properties: Love, attraction, binding, empowerment, control, fidelity, lust.

Health Properties: Treats heartburn, soothes sore throats, stops coughs, protects against cavities, treats hot flashes.

Medical Warnings: Do not consume licorice root in large doses over a long period of time. Do not take if you are pregnant and/or breastfeeding. Do not take if you are on blood-pressure medicine, blood thinners, cholesterol-lowering medicine, diuretics, estrogen-based birth control, or NSAIDs.

MUGWORT

A staple item in any witch's herbal cabinet, mugwort has always had a mystical history. Its botanical name, *Artemisia vulgaris*, was chosen in honor of the Greek goddess Artemis and is associated with the lunar cycle and women's health. For years it has been used for medicine, from regulating menstrual cycles to easing menopause. Fun fact: beer used to be made with mugwort until hops became popular.

What It Looks Like: Mugwort looks a lot like a weed, so be careful not to accidentally brew ragweed into your tea. Its leaves are dark green on top, but underneath they are silver and covered in wooly hairs. When dried, mugwort turns a light brown.

Flavor Profile: Bitter.

Magical Properties: Divination, psychic dreaming, protection, spiritual cleansing, associated with the moon.

Health Properties: Regulates menstrual cycles, calming, diuretic, boosts energy, aids digestion, promotes circulation, supports liver health, alleviates sore muscles.

Medical Warnings: Do not use if you are pregnant or have allergies to ragweed, carrots, or celery.

NUTMEG

A holiday favorite found in everything from pumpkin spice lattes to the topping of our favorite glass of eggnog. However, did you know that nutmeg has plenty of magical power within it as well, other than the power to make us crave it every holiday season?

What It Looks Like: Nutmeg is an oval-shaped seed from a nutmeg tree native to Indonesia. The seed is brown and about an inch long, with a lace-like substance that covers it. Nutmeg is available as a ground spice or whole seed that you can grate yourself.

Flavor Profile: Nutty and sweet.

Magical Properties: Luck, legal justice, travel, lucid dreaming, attraction, encourages psychic visions, prosperity.

Health Properties: Relieves arthritis pain, boosts sex drive, prevents gum disease, boosts mood, improves memory, increases heart health.

Medical Warnings: Nutmeg can cause hallucinations and loss of coordination if you consume too much of it.

PASSIONFLOWER

One of the most unique and magical-looking flowers, the passionflower looks like something out of a fantasy novel or spell book. Native to the southern United States, passionflowers were used by the Algonquin tribe and the Cherokee. Spanish missionaries gave the flower the name "passionflower" as it reminded them of the crucifixion, or "passion" (originally meaning "suffering"), of Christ. The petals and leaves of the passionflower are great for teas, tinctures, and herbal infusions.

What It Looks Like: Passionflowers are vines that climb with tendrils or stay on the ground. The flower is highly recognizable with its wavy lavender petals and its visible pistil (that produces seeds) and stamen (that holds the pollen), which are located outside of the flower in the center.

Flavor Profile: Mild flavor that has a grassy earthiness to it.

Magical Properties: Friendship, relaxation, good luck, love, calm, peace, sleep.

Health Properties: Helps with severe anxiety, decreases muscle tension, calms nerves, helps with headaches, stops sleep difficulties.

Medical Warnings: Do not take with a sedative or if you are pregnant or breastfeeding.

PEPPERMINT

A wintertime favorite. You know the holiday season is here when almost everything becomes peppermint flavored. However, there's actually a more mystical energy in your peppermint mocha besides holiday magic. Peppermint is one of the most popular flavors to add to tea for its taste and abilities to soothe a sore throat, among other things. Not a fan of minty flavors but want the same magical and healing benefits? Check out spearmint, which has a lighter, sweeter taste because it contains less menthol than peppermint.

What It Looks Like: Peppermint has square stems with smooth, dark-green leaves. In late summer, violet flowers appear in tiny clusters around the stem. You can use dried or fresh peppermint leaves, but fresh is best.

Flavor Profile: Minty.

Magical Properties: Luck, positive thoughts, inspiration, divination, prosperity, cleansing, healing, mental clarity, protection.

Health Properties: Eases tension headaches; reduces nasal congestion; helps ease bloating, nausea, and gas; helps reduce upper respiratory infections; reduces seasonal allergies; soothes sore throats; boosts energy.

Medical Warnings: None.

RASPBERRY LEAF

When enjoying freshly picked raspberries, don't be so quick to throw away those leaves; they have magical properties to them, along with healing benefits. Dried out, raspberry leaves can be added to teas for a magical (especially romance) boost. You can also use regular raspberries in teas, either fresh, dried, or infused in a syrup.

What It Looks Like: Raspberry leaves are pale green with seven leaflets attached to raspberries on a shrub.

Flavor Profile: Fruity, floral, and dessert-like.

Magical Properties: Confidence, attraction, joy, protection, healing. Associated with fairies.

BERRY LEAVES

Raspberry, blackberry, and strawberry leaf all have special magical and health benefits, stemming from the magical and healing properties of the berries they come from. In folk magic, very little is wasted, and each part of a fruit or herb has a magical property that can be used. While it's not very tempting to chew on some leaves, they can be a tasty addition in teas or useful in spells where you don't want to waste the actual fruit but want to add in the plant's magical benefits.

Health Properties: Relieves cramps, eases labor pains, induces labor, increases milk production, boosts metabolism.

Medical Warnings: Only use in the third trimester when pregnant. Talk to your doctor if you're sensitive to the effects of estrogen as raspberry leaf mimics estrogen in the body.

ROOIBOS

Rooibos, which translates as "red bush," is a plant found in South Africa. Rooibos "tea" is made from the leaves of a shrub called *Aspalathus linearis*. Rooibos is quickly becoming a popular addition in most tea blends, and its magical powers cannot be beat.

What It Looks Like: Despite being called "red bush," the shrub that rooibos comes from isn't actually red. The plant has green, needle-like leaves with small yellow flowers. It develops a reddish color when the leaves are fermented.

Flavor Profile: Smooth, sweet flavor with a hint of vanilla.

Magical Properties: Strength, courage, determination, patience, rejuvenation, inner peace, energy, grounding, dreamwork.

Health Properties: Increases heart health, good for healthy skin, rich in antioxidants, improves digestion and bone health.

Medical Warnings: People who are undergoing chemotherapy should avoid taking rooibos in large amounts. It also can act like estrogen in the body, so if you are trying to lower your estrogen levels for any reason, avoid rooibos.

ROSE

The staple of Valentine's Day, anniversary presents, and "I'm sorry" gifts, roses are one of the most popular flowers and are used in everything from skincare products to baked goods. Rose is also a classic ingredient in many spells and potions, from love spells to healing draughts, making it a must-have in every witch's cabinet.

What It Looks Like: Contrary to popular belief, roses don't have thorns; they have prickles that are on the outer layer of the stem (though, in fairness to Brett Michaels, "Every Rose Has Its Prickles" doesn't have the same ring to it). Roses come in various shapes, containing many petals tucked into a cup shape and standing straight up. Roses also come in many colors, from the common reds, pinks, and whites, to yellow, orange, blue, and black. The colors have a magical correspondence, so keep that in mind when spell casting and brewing. The "fruit" of the rose plant is called the rose hip, and can also be used in tea and other spells. The rose hip is usually red or orange and is round in shape.

Flavor Profile: Sweet and fruity, similar to strawberry and green apple.

Magical Properties: Divination, fortune, healing, love, psychic abilities, compassion, good luck, protection, beauty, glamour, calming.

Health Properties: Good for decreasing anxiety, relieves menstrual pain, anti-inflammatory, improves heart health, reduces stress, provides a mental boost. It's also great for the skin.

Medical Warnings: Do not use rose-scented skin products if you are allergic to roses, are on blood thinners, or are taking antidepressants.

STAR ANISE

This very recognizable spice is a key ingredient in Chinese five-spice powder and Indian garam masala (a spice blend) and a variety of soups, desserts, and teas. However, before being used as a popular cooking spice, star anise was used for centuries to heal illnesses, especially digestive and lung issues. It also has strong magical benefits. Many use the spice as a pendulum when doing readings for a psychic boost.

What It Looks Like: Star anise is so named because it's shaped like a star; well, its seedpods are shaped like stars. Star anise comes from the fruit of a shrub; these are harvested just before they ripen and are then dried in the sun, giving them their dark brown, reddish-orange color. They can be used whole or ground.

Flavor Profile: Sweet, similar to licorice.

Magical Properties: Psychic powers, luck, happiness, protection, dreams.

Health Properties: Relieves digestive issues like gas, bloating, and cramping; calms the nerves; aids sleep; can relieve cough, bronchitis, and asthma.

Medical Warnings: Do not give to infants or small children. While star anise is safe for most adults, it looks very similar to Japanese star anise, which is actually poisonous. Make sure you get your star anise from a reputable place so you won't have that confusion.

STRAWBERRY LEAF

While we typically just cut these off our strawberries, be mindful before you throw those leaves away; they actually have a lot of magical benefits. Herbalists have been using the benefits of strawberries for improving the heart but and for bringing love and fertility.

What It Looks Like: Strawberry leaf consists of green leaves found in groups of three with serrated edges.

Flavor Profile: Mild fruity flavor with grassy notes.

Magical Properties: Love, luck, friendship, happiness.

Health Properties: Rich in antioxidants, boosts the immune system, regulates blood sugar, improves heart health.

Medical Warnings: Can cause cramping, upset stomach, and constipation. Do not consume if you are on blood thinners.

THYME

What thyme is it? It's herb thyme! Puns aside (for now), thyme is a wonderful, versatile herb that is easy to access; both fresh and ground thyme can be found at your local grocery store. You can easily grow your own thyme in a garden or on your kitchen windowsill. Used by the ancient Egyptians as part of their embalming practice, thyme has also been used for thousands of years for healing purposes, from treating wounds to preventing nightmares. Basically, you can use thyme for almost everything.

What It Looks Like: There are three different types of thyme: English, German, and French. English and French thyme have pointy green leaves with red stems, while German thyme has round green leaves with green stems.

Flavor Profile: Grassy, floral notes.

Magical Properties: Manifesting, attraction, love magic, glamour, prosperity, multiplying, smoothing things over.

Health Properties: Stimulates appetite; boosts the immune system; decreases anxiety; helps with chest infections, colds, sore throats, coughs, and urinary tract infections; relieves menstrual cramps.

Medical Warnings: Do not take in large quantities if you have a bleeding disorder, are scheduled for surgery, or are on blood thinners. Because thyme acts like estrogen in the body, try to avoid it if you have breast cancer, uterine cancer, ovarian cancer, endometriosis, or uterine fibroids.

TURMERIC

One of the main spices in curry, turmeric is quickly becoming one of the most popular add-ins in teas and just about everything else. Its popularity comes from its health benefits: the root contains a yellow chemical called curcumin, which can heal various ills (see below). A common culinary spice in India, Southeast Asia, and the Middle East, it has been used in India for centuries as medicine.

What It Looks Like: Fresh turmeric looks similar to ginger, only its inside flesh is bright orange. When ground, it keeps its orange color.

Flavor Profile: Warm, bitter taste.

Magical Properties: Protection, health, fertility, banishment.

Health Properties: Boosts brain development, improves memory, relieves heartburn, lowers the risk of heart disease, eases arthritis pain, eases depression symptoms, promotes longevity, reduces hay fever symptoms.

Medical Warnings: Do not take if you have gallbladder issues, a bleeding disorder, endometriosis, uterine fibroids, an iron deficiency, or breast, uterine, or ovarian cancer. Do not take two weeks before surgery.

YERBA MATE

This South American herb is truly magical: it has the strength of coffee, the pleasure of chocolate, and the health benefits of tea. Witchcraft, I tell you! Yerba mate is known as the herb of the gods because it was first consumed by the Guarani tribe of Brazil. They believed that the herb was one of the reincarnations of the god Caá Yarîi. In South American countries, yerba mate is usually drunk out of a gourd through a metal straw called a "bombilla" and shared with friends.

What It Looks Like: Yerba mate comes from the yerba mate tree, which has dark green leaves with greenish flowers. The leaves and twigs of the tree are dried and chopped or ground to make tea.

Flavor Profile: Earthy with a grassy finish and slightly bitter.

Magical Properties: Friendship, bonding, creativity, insight, attraction.

Health Properties: Rich in antioxidants, boosts physical and mental energy, improves mental focus, stops dandruff, boosts metabolism, lowers blood sugar levels.

Medical Warnings: Yerba mate contains caffeine, so do not drink if you have caffeine sensitivities, if you are taking antidepressants or Parkinson's medication, or if you are pregnant.

OTHER INGREDIENTS TO HAVE ON HAND

While these are not strictly herbs, teas, or spices, you will need some other ingredients to have in your witchy cabinet to enhance the magic, the flavor, or both. Here's what to stock up on to add to your teas when desired.

COCOA NIBS: Grounding, prosperity, happiness, connecting to the spiritual world.

HONEY: Sweetness, abundance, motivation, healing, happiness, fairies, self-love, prosperity, mending friendships, relationships, protection, attraction, glamour magic, manifestation.

LEMON (PEEL OR JUICE): Awareness, energy, love, love magic, the sun, purification, hexing.

ORANGE PEEL: Divination, love, luck.

PEPPERCORN: Relieves energy blocks, promotes psychic ability, protection, strength, confidence.

SUGAR: Manifesting, attraction, love magic, glamour, prosperity, multiplying, smoothing things over, and increasing receptiveness to ideas.

VANILLA (BEAN OR EXTRACT): Love, passion, vitality, happiness, healing, friendship, luck, mental quickness, beauty, relieves stress.

WHERE SHOULD I GET MY HERBS?

Fresh is best! Just like in cooking and baking, it's ideal to use fresh ingredients in all of your brews. Fresh herbs, teas, and spices will help you achieve not only the best taste but also the most potent magical benefits. However, this doesn't mean you have to spend a ton of money to get the "best" green tea or very expensive cinnamon for your spells to work. Nor does it mean you have to start your own garden. If you are a witch on a budget or have limited resources, use what you can. As Ina Garten says, store-bought is fine.

Having said that, as with most things in witchcraft, our intent is just as important as the ingredients we use and the spells we cast, so we need to be mindful. Most of the teas and spices we use have a very violent history of colonialism, imperialism, and the exploitation of human beings, and this violent legacy is still alive today. The rising popularity of witchcraft has brought on an increase in cultural appropriation. This has led to the overharvesting and abuse of treasured medicine and religious plants of India, Africa, China, South America, and the indigenous tribes of North America. So please, honor these ingredients and treat them with care. When possible, buy your ingredients directly from small businesses that grow and harvest herbs ethically. Capitalism has made it nearly impossible to completely avoid dealing with industries that get rich off of abusing human lives and spiritual practices for money. Even buying just one herb or spice locally or from someone of that traditional cultural heritage can make a difference.

Chapter 3

WITCH'S BREWS: TEA AND POTIONS FOR EVERY OCCASION

A potion is a spell that can be consumed. When crafting our potions, we carefully add different ingredients to create a desirable outcome, whether we are putting honey in our green tea to heal a sore throat or adding lavender to a brew for protection. There are many ways you can create your own tea or herbal blend. You can go all out and grow and dry your own herbs and then blend them together with mortar and pestle. You can purchase herbs from small businesses, or you can combine store-bought teas and infuse the rest with an infuser. Find the technique that works for you, even if you have to do a little trial and error.

WATER: TEA'S SECRET INGREDIENT

Next to the tea itself, the second most important ingredient in any tea blend is the water—it's what makes tea, tea! So, you should be mindful of the water you use. That's not to say that you should run out and buy expensive bottles of sparkling water, but tap water from the sink, heated up in the microwave, isn't going to cut it. That's because tap water and well water are filled with hard-water substances, changing the alchemy in your brew. And when you put water in the microwave, you get all the different smells from previously heated food infused into your water, changing the flavor. For the most tasty and magical tea, use distilled water heated up in a kettle.

INFUSING MAGIC INTO YOUR WATER

You can also charge your water using the sun, the moon, or even crystals. Charging is using an external source of energy, usually organic, to power your item or infuse the quality of the energy source into your item. You can use water infused with the sun, the moon, or crystals to put some extra magic into your potions.

SUN WATER

Place your cup of water in the sun (for instance, on a windowsill or anywhere it can feel the warmth of the sun) for a few moments. If you want to make a lot of sun water to have for later, you can fill a mason jar or a pitcher with water, place it in the sun for an hour, and store it for later. Sun water's magical properties include happiness, positivity, and energy.

MOON WATER

Follow the same basic process described for making sun water. Place your water where it can reflect the moon's light. However, because the moon cycles through phases, it's particularly important to know what moon phase you're charging your water under. New moon water is very different from full moon water.

 NEW MOON WATER: New beginnings, setting intentions, new projects.

 FULL MOON WATER: Calming, manifesting, letting things go, major energy.

If you want to charge your water under a different moon phase, check Chapters Five and Six to learn more about the lunar phases and what each phase represents.

CRYSTAL WATER

You can infuse the power and energy of crystals into your water, either by putting a crystal into water and letting it sit overnight or by placing crystals around your container of water.

NOTE: Some crystals cannot go into water, so make sure you do some research before plopping crystals into your water.

Here are some ideas to get you started:

ROSE QUARTZ WATER: Healing, relaxation, calming, self-love.

🔮 **AMETHYST WATER:** Protection, spiritual wisdom, divination, purifying.

🔮 **CITRINE WATER:** Motivation, creativity, emotional balance.

🔮 **MOONSTONE WATER:** Intuition, balance, wishes.

STIRRING THE TEA

It's important to have a spoon on hand during your tea and potion-making—and not just to stir in additional ingredients like honey or sugar. The spoon acts as a magic wand of sorts, bringing your magic to life. Some people like to use a spoon with a crystal (usually amethyst or some type of quartz) on the handle, but any old kitchen spoon will do. The real magic comes from how you stir, as this decides how the spell will work out.

CLOCKWISE: Stirring your drink clockwise to invoke, or wake up, your magic; infusing your brew with positive energy and intentions. This is meant to attract good vibes like beauty, energy, wealth, and healing.

COUNTERCLOCKWISE: Stirring your drink counterclockwise will banish any negative energy or bad vibes from you as you stir, acting almost as protection. This is great for reducing anxiety or banishing people from your life.

THE RULE OF THREE: Throughout this book, we will be using the number three a lot: stirring your brew three times, saying spells three times, etc. This is because three is a powerful number in witchcraft. It represents the triple goddess (maid, mother, and crone). In certain neopagan practice, one must perform three tasks (one for each goddess) in order to earn their favor and grant their wish or help in the witch's spell. In Wicca, three represents the rule of three, which states that what you put out into the world will come back to you threefold, good and bad. So, when in doubt, do it in threes.

Here are some tea and potion recipes for every occasion.

ANTI ANXIE-TEA

Whether you start the morning with knots in your stomach or are nervously waiting for a phone call or important meeting; whether the daily news is filling you with dread or you deal with anxiety regularly, this potion will make coping with anxiety a little easier. With zero caffeine, this blend is great to make in advance for stressful days, whether you start your day with it, have one at night, or sip whenever you need to calm down.

---

1 teaspoon dried passionflower (*anxiety-reducing, decreases muscle tension, good luck*)

1 teaspoon dried rose petals (*self-love, protection*)

½ teaspoon dried lavender (*relaxation, healing, happiness boost*)

3 drops lemon juice (*awareness*)

1 cup hot water

honey, to taste (*healing and self-love*)

INSTRUCTIONS

Put the passionflower, rose petals, and lavender into a tea infuser (or loose into a teacup if you are planning to read). Place the infuser (if using) into a large mug. Add the lemon. Pour the hot water into the cup or mug and add honey. Allow the tea to steep for 10 minutes. Remove the infuser and stir clockwise. Close your eyes and take a deep breath, counting down from ten before taking your first sip.

FOR A DASH OF MAGIC

🜨 Use pink dried rose petals as pink roses are associated with gentleness and peace.

🜨 To add a little more comfort and ease, perform the "Everything Will Be Alright" spell on page 138 before drinking.

🜨 If you are nervous before starting your day, perform "The Daily Forecast" ritual on page 96 to get a look at your day ahead. You can also drink this before the "Should I Be Worried?" reading on page 116 to get an idea of what you don't need to fret about.

GOOD-THYME TEA

While this tea is perfect for hot summer days spent chilling on the beach with your coven, it can also be used on rainy days and snowy winter mornings when you want to feel a little sunshine to combat the winter blues. This brew is great for boosting happiness and providing a sense of security, like you're on summer vacation without a care in the world. It can be served hot or cold, depending on your vibe.

---

1 teaspoon black tea *(energy, mental clarity, grounding)*
½ teaspoon dried or fresh thyme *(kindness, self-love, prosperity)*
½ teaspoon dried blueberries *(happiness, releases inhibitions, wishes)*
1 cup hot water
1 lemon peel *(happiness, energy)*

INSTRUCTIONS

Place the black tea, thyme, and dried blueberries into a tea infuser (or loose into your teacup if you are planning to read). Place the infuser into your cup. Pour in the hot water and let it steep for 3 minutes. (If you are making iced tea with this, take the infuser out and place in the refrigerator to cool.) Add the lemon peel and stir clockwise before enjoying.

FOR A DASH OF MAGIC

🌀 Place the water you will be using in the sun for an hour to charge it. Sun-charged water brings happiness and energy to your brew.

🌀 Use this tea with the "Good Vibes Only Spell" on page 141 to really double those good energies.

🌀 Draw a sigil for happiness on the bottom of your cup for good energy. See page 134 for more on sigil magic.

THE MIDAS BLEND

In Greek mythology, King Midas was a wealthy king who did a favor for the party god, Dionysus. When Dionysus asked the king what he wanted in return for this favor, Midas replied, "I wish for everything I touch to become gold." While things didn't work out well for poor Midas, we all hope for the "Midas touch" at some point in our lives: success in business, creative opportunities, or just more money in general. This blend will help you manifest what you desire, making everything you touch turn to gold. No worries—it's not literal this time!

---

1 teaspoon **white tea** (*new beginnings, psychic ability, manifestation*)
1 teaspoon **dried dandelion root** (*wishes granted, good luck*)
1 teaspoon **dried lemon balm** (*success, money*)
½ teaspoon **ground ginger** (*quick manifestation*)
1 cup **hot water**

INSTRUCTIONS

Put the white tea, dandelion root, lemon balm, and ground ginger into a tea infuser (or loose into a teacup if you plan to read). Place the infuser into a mug. Pour in the hot water and let steep for 7 minutes. While you wait, gaze into your cup or mug and visualize what you want to have more of in your life (more money, projects becoming successful, a job opportunity, successful dates, etc.). When the tea has steeped, take your spoon and stir clockwise three times and then tap the center of the cup; this is your "magic touch."

FOR A DASH OF MAGIC

🌙 Use water for the tea that has been charged under the new moon. New moon water is perfect for manifesting as the moon is just beginning the lunar cycle.

🌙 If you want to add some extra attraction, use the "Come to Me" spell on page 136.

🌙 For best results, make this tea on a Sunday, as it is the best day for success spells and brews.

🌙 For an extra boost of confidence about getting what you want, use the "More Powerful Than You Could Ever Know" spell on page 147.

THIRD EYE OPENER

Every single person has the ability to see into the future. It's the intuition we are all born with, though it goes by many names: ESP, the sixth sense, psychic awareness, and the third eye. The third eye (also known as the sixth chakra) is your invisible eye, located between your eyebrows, that helps you see past the physical realm and into the metaphysical. Some people are born with the ability to open their third eye with ease, but for others, it's going to take a little more work. This tea will help you open your third eye, so drink this when doing a tea reading or tarot, or when you have a big decision to make. The recipe features blue cornflower, which is associated with the third eye chakra for its intuitive qualities and its vibrant indigo color, the same color as the chakra.

1½ teaspoons oolong tea *(divination, psychic awareness)*
½ teaspoon dried peppermint *(enhancing the third eye)*
½ teaspoon fresh or dried blue cornflower
(psychic insight, self-knowledge, accessing inner wisdom)
1 cup hot water

INSTRUCTIONS

Put the oolong tea, peppermint, and blue cornflower into a tea infuser (or loose into a teacup if you are planning to read), and place the infuser, if using, into a mug. Pour in the hot water and let it steep for 4 minutes; it should turn a lovely indigo color. As you wait for it to steep, take a moment to close your eyes and meditate for a few moments. When your tea finishes steeping, take out the infuser (if using) and stir your tea three times, clockwise. As you drink, close your eyes and visualize your third eye opening up.

FOR A DASH OF MAGIC

- If you want to have psychic dreams, add ½ teaspoon of dried mugwort into the blend and drink just before bed.
- Place a sigil for divination under your cup. This will give you an extra boost of intuition (see Chapter Six for sigil magic information).
- Take a piece of star anise and tie a piece of string or floss around it and use it for pendulum dowsing (see Chapter Seven for pendulum dowsing).
- Use this tea if you are doing tasseography or other types of divination: tarot, runes, pendulum reading, etc.
- For best results, brew this on a Monday as it is the best day for divination.
- Charge your brew with an amethyst crystal, or make the tea with amethyst-infused water for an extra psychic boost.

LOVE POTION NO. 9

Yes, the classic love potion, one of the most sought-after brews in witchcraft. It was actually one of the first brews I ever tried making. Call me a hopeless romantic, but I don't know one witch who doesn't have their own special love potion. Drink this when you are ready to welcome love into your life, when you're scrolling through dating apps, or when you just need a little self-love.

A note on consent: Love potions have been a subject of discussion among the magical community due to the lack of consent in "forcing" someone to fall in love with you. I believe it depends on the situation. If you are looking to welcome love into your life and try to attract it (as this potion is intended to do), then a love potion is fine. However, if you are drinking it to try to get a particular person to fall in love with you—or worse, make them drink it without telling them what it is, that's a hard NO. Also, forcing someone to fall in love with you is never worth it in the long run. You will ultimately discover that the person is not right for you or is a total jerk, giving you more of a headache than joy. So, when drinking this, try to manifest the person who is right for you, not the person you think is right for you.

1 teaspoon white tea *(new beginnings, happiness)*
1 teaspoon fresh or dried rose petals *(glamour, love)*
½ teaspoon dried raspberry leaf *(love, passion, happiness)*
½ teaspoon dried lemon balm *(strong attraction, love)*
dash of pure vanilla extract *(passion, love, happiness)*
1 cup hot water

INSTRUCTIONS

Put the white tea, rose petals, raspberry leaf, lemon balm, and vanilla into a tea infuser (or loose into a teacup if you plan on reading), and place the infuser into a cup. Pour in the hot water and allow it to steep for 5 minutes. As it steeps, close your eyes and invoke the feelings of love—how does love make you feel? Warm and fuzzy? Excited? Comforted? Recall these feelings while holding the cup. When the tea has steeped, remove the infuser and stir three times. As you drink, scroll through dating apps, flirt with people, or just keep invoking those loving vibes.

FOR A DASH OF MAGIC

Add some honey to your tea for self-love.

Add a little bit of sugar if you want a lot of love in your life, as sugar is associated with multiplying. However, be careful with it; you don't want so many suitors knocking on your door that it becomes overwhelming.

Use water infused with rose quartz for some extra self-love and romantic vibes.

Use this tea when doing the "Who Is My Next Lover?" reading on page 109, or any general love reading. Just switch out the white tea with oolong to see the leaves better.

 Drink this tea after doing the "Love Me, Love Me" spell on page 161 to increase your love and attraction energy.

 Brew this tea on a Friday as Friday is ruled by Venus, which makes it perfect for love potions.

NEGATIVE THOUGHT REPELLENT

Some days are more challenging than others. You hear a little voice in your head that tells you all the negative things, and it can leave you rattled, scared, and doubting yourself. Well, for those days when the mean voice just won't stop talking, here's a brew that will quiet it a little.

1½ teaspoons black tea *(banishing bad thoughts)*
1 teaspoon rose hips *(self-love)*
1 teaspoon dried lemon balm *(healing from past negativity)*
¼ teaspoon dried chamomile *(inner calm and peace)*
¼ teaspoon peppermint *(bringing in positive thoughts)*
1 cup hot water

INSTRUCTIONS

Put the black tea, rose hips, lemon balm, chamomile, and peppermint into a tea infuser (or loose into your cup if you plan on reading), and place the infuser into your cup. Pour the hot water into the cup and let it steep for 5 minutes. After the tea has steeped, take your spoon and stir counterclockwise three times. As you stir, picture all those negative thoughts being banished from your mind and from the world. Drink and let that mean voice be silenced.

FOR A DASH OF MAGIC

 Put in a little honey for some extra self-love.

 Pair this tea with the "Everything Will Be Alright" spell on page 138 for some extra reassurance.

 As you're drinking your tea, take out a piece of paper and draw a line down the middle, dividing it in half. On the left, write down all of your negative thoughts. On the right, write how that negative thought is not based in reality or spin it into a positive. For example, the thought "everyone hates me" can be broken into "I have lots of friends that love and care about me, like . . ." and name your friends and loved ones.

 Write comforting mantras while drinking your tea, and repeat them to yourself.

CREATIVI-TEA

Feeling stuck in a creative rut? Unable to conjure anything from a piece of art to a simple spell? This is the tea for writers, artists, musicians, and creators of all kinds, for when you're suffering through that dreaded creative block when *nothing* comes out. This tea will help increase your imagination, banish mental blocks, and boost your energy so you can become inspired, motivated, and ready to create your masterpiece.

---

1 teaspoon green tea *(energy boost, passion)*

½ teaspoon dried ginger *(clarity, energy boost, confidence, manifestation, passion, power, success)*

½ teaspoon dried lemon verbena *(creativity)*

1 teaspoon dried spearmint *(clarity, inspiration, positive thoughts, prosperity)*

¼ teaspoon dried elderflower *(new beginnings, prosperity)*

1 cup hot water

dash of honey *(abundance, motivation, manifestation, prosperity)*

INSTRUCTIONS

For best results, make this tea in the same place where you usually do your creative work: at your desk, in your art studio, in your bed, or wherever you do your best work. Put the green tea, ginger, lemon verbena, spearmint, and elderflower in your tea infuser and place the infuser into your cup. Pour in the hot water and let it steep for seven minutes. As it steeps, gather your creative supplies: notebook, pen, pencils, sketchbook, canvas, paints, or whatever tools you use to create. After your tea has steeped, stir in the honey three times clockwise with your spoon. As you drink, allowing your mind to wander, don't focus on any particular thing or force yourself to be creative. Just let yourself drift and see where your mind goes. When you feel an idea come or just have a feeling of inspiration, grab your pen or paintbrush and get to work! Don't think about it; just go with the feeling and see what you come up with.

FOR A DASH OF MAGIC

 Pair this blend with the "Come to Me" spell on page 136 to bring some extra inspiration to you.

This may not be the best blend to use for a tea reading. While it may help increase your imagination to tell a story, the tea may become *too* creative and give you a totally out-there reading that sounds more like science fiction than real life. However, it can be useful if you're having trouble with writer's block and do tea reading for story ideas.

The best day to use this spell is Wednesday, as Wednesday is ruled by Mercury, the planet of communication.

BASIC WITCH BREW

Everyone knows that pumpkin spice is a witch's brew, and not only because it shows up every autumn—the witchiest season. It's also because it contains a combination of herbs and spices that gives you a boost of everything a modern witch needs: courage, energy, creativity, success, happiness, protection, and a little bit of luck. That pumpkin spice latte you've been drinking? A magic potion. So if you're looking for a dash of magic year-round, check out this basically delicious brew.

1½ teaspoons rooibos *(energy boost, courage)*

⅓ teaspoon ground cinnamon *(happiness, creativity)*

½ teaspoon fresh or dried ginger *(confidence, success)*

¼ teaspoon whole cloves *(protection)*

⅓ teaspoon ground nutmeg *(luck, wealth, psychic power, attraction)*

2 pieces star anise *(success)*

1 cup hot water

INSTRUCTIONS

Put the rooibos, cinnamon, ginger, cloves, nutmeg, and star anise into your infuser (or loose into your teacup if you're planning to read), and place the infuser into your cup. Pour in the hot water and let steep for 5 minutes. Stir clockwise three times. Drink and stay magical, witches!

FOR A DASH OF MAGIC

🌀 If you would like to use this blend for tea readings, swap out the rooibos with 1½ teaspoons of black tea.

🌀 For divination, tie a piece of star anise to a string and hover it over the cup to do some pendulum dowsing.

🌀 For a magical boost, pair this tea with the "More Powerful Than You Could Ever Know" spell on page 147.

ELIXIR OF GLAMOUR

Glamour magic has always been popular in traditional and modern witchcraft—though there's always been a slight misunderstanding about the art. No, glamour won't transform you into an entirely different person overnight, nor will it radically change the features on your face and/or body that you're less than happy with. However, this glamorous brew *will* give you a boost of confidence, bring out your natural beauty, and have people drawn to your own unique looks. Not to mention that drinking this often will help improve your skin and hair. Drink this before a big date, while getting ready, or when you just want to boost your appearance a bit.

---

1 teaspoon rooibos *(rejuvenation, glowing skin, inner peace)*

1 teaspoon ground ginseng *(beauty, vitality)*

½ teaspoon fresh or dried thyme *(attraction, glamour)*

½ teaspoon dried hibiscus flowers
(glamour, relaxation, healthy hair)

pinch of coconut flakes *(confidence)*

1 cup hot water

INSTRUCTIONS

Put the rooibos, ginseng, thyme, hibiscus, and coconut flakes into your tea infuser (or loose into your cup if you plan on reading), and place the infuser into your cup. Pour in the hot water and let it steep for 4 minutes. Stir clockwise three times. As you sip, begin to do your glamour ritual: doing your hair and makeup, picking out an outfit, painting your nails, taking selfies, whatever! Drink whenever you need a little boost of glamour.

FOR A DASH OF MAGIC

 If you want to drink this before a big date or just want to add dental care to your beauty routine, replace the coconut flakes with a ½ teaspoon dried peppermint for fresh breath.

 Drink this before or after performing the "Love Me, Love Me" spell for an extra boost of self-love.

 The best day to perform this spell is Friday as it is ruled by Venus, the goddess of love and beauty.

 For an extra bit of magic, brew this potion in a lavender-colored cup as the color lavender is associated with beauty.

CONFIDENCE IN A CUP

Even the most powerful witches need a little extra boost of confidence every once in a while. When fear is making you pause—whether you are facing a job interview, a first date, or something important you must say or do—this tea will help you do what you have to do with confidence, courage, and a dash of luck.

1½ teaspoons Earl Grey tea *(the bergamot oil in the Earl Grey blend brings confidence, self-acceptance, optimism, hope, and self-worth, while the black tea brings courage, energy boost, and strength)*

½ teaspoon raspberry leaf *(confidence, protection)*

½ teaspoon licorice root *(control, power)*

¼ teaspoon ground cinnamon *(luck, success)*

1 cup hot water

dash of honey *(motivation, manifestation)*

INSTRUCTIONS

Put the Earl Grey tea, raspberry leaf, licorice root, and cinnamon into your infuser (or loose into your cup if you're planning to read), and place the infuser into your cup. Pour in the hot water and wait 4 minutes for the tea to steep. Pour in the honey and stir clockwise three times. As you drink, allow the power and confidence to flow through you. You're ready to take on the world!

FOR A DASH OF MAGIC

 If you're curious about how your day is going to go, do the "Daily Forecast" ritual reading on page 96 to get some extra confidence about the day ahead.

 If you're hoping that your newfound confidence will help you attract the things you want in life, use the "Come to Me" spell on page 136.

 Use the "More Powerful Than You Could Ever Know" spell on page 147 for a double shot of confidence.

 Use the "Everything Will Be Alright" spell on page 138 if you need some extra reassurance that things will go your way.

SWEET DREAMS DRAUGHT

When you can't fall asleep, this draught will help calm the mind by promoting inner peace, relieving stress, and putting positive thoughts in your head so you can slide into dreamland with ease.

———————— ❊ ————————

1 teaspoon dried lavender *(calming, rest, good dreams)*
½ teaspoon dried passionflower *(calming, peace)*
1 teaspoon dried spearmint *(positive thoughts)*
½ teaspoon dried lemon verbena *(protection from nightmares)*
1 cup hot water

———————— ❊ ————————

INSTRUCTIONS

Right before bed, put the lavender, passionflower, spearmint, and lemon verbena in your tea infuser and place it in your cup. Pour in the hot water and let it steep for 5 minutes. While this steeps, go about your bedtime routine. When the blend has finished steeping, stir three times with a spoon. If possible, bring the tea into bed with you and sip while doing something relaxing: reading a book, listening to some calming music, meditating, etc. Try to avoid using technology; it'll just keep you up. Drink and prepare for sweet dreams.

FOR A DASH OF MAGIC

🜂 If you want to trade sweet dreams for psychic dreams, add ½ teaspoon of dried mugwort to your blend.

🜂 Perform the "Let Me F*cking Sleep" spell on page 153 to help yourself get to sleep.

🜂 Modify this into a hot chocolate recipe by taking out the lemon verbena and adding in hot chocolate. Simply prepare the hot chocolate as you typically would (either stirred in a pot or made with a hot chocolate packet). Then, put the rest of the ingredients in an infuser and let steep for five minutes.

🜂 Write a sigil for a restful night's sleep. Place it either at the bottom of the cup or under your pillow (see page 134 for more on sigil magic).

🜂 Place an amethyst crystal by your bed for positive dreams.

SAFE-TEA FIRST

The world can be a pretty spooky place—and not the fun kind of spooky. We could all use a little extra protection in life, whether we are home alone, going to a new place for the first time, or just don't feel as safe as we wish to be. This tea blend will act as a guard to protect you from harm (from toxic people to harmful spirits), banish bad energy, and help you put your mind at ease. It will also make you alert enough that if trouble *does* go down, you'll be prepared. This blend has many different variations depending on your safe-tea needs, so check the "For a Dash of Magic" section below for more possibilities.

Note: Remember, this tea is meant to give you another layer of protection, not to act as your only form of protection, so make sure you continue your other magical and non-magical safety measures to protect yourself: lock your doors, make sure to tell someone where you are if you're traveling by yourself, don't take drinks from strangers, etc.

---

1 teaspoon vanilla-flavored black tea or black tea with vanilla extract (*the black tea provides courage, grounding, stability, and banishment of bad energy, while the vanilla relieves stress and increases mental quickness*)

½ teaspoon dried elderflower (*protection, calming*)

1 teaspoon dried chamomile (*peace, protection*)

½ teaspoon dried lemongrass (*warding off negative energy*)

1 cup hot water

INSTRUCTIONS

First, put a salt circle around you or the cup, if possible, to add another layer of protection. Put the vanilla black tea, elderflower, chamomile, and lemongrass into your infuser and place into your cup. Pour in the hot water and let it steep for 5 minutes. As the tea steeps, visualize yourself being perfectly safe, like you have a barrier that surrounds you, keeping you away from harm. Hold that image in your mind's eye. When the tea is finished steeping, stir three times counterclockwise to banish the harmful energy. Then stir three more times clockwise, saying with each stir, "I am safe, I am protected, I am secure." Drink and feel yourself being shielded from harm.

FOR A DASH OF MAGIC

If you need legal protection, replace the chamomile with dried calendula.

If you need spiritual protection, add in 1 teaspoon of dried spearmint.

If you need protection from illness or evil, use Earl Grey tea instead of vanilla-flavored black tea.

If you're looking to feel safe at home, add fresh or dried blueberries or put in a few drops of blueberry flavoring.

Place a protection sigil on the bottom of your cup or on a piece of paper under your mug for an extra dose of protection (see page 134 for more on sigil magic).

Before brewing your tea, cleanse your space by doing a smoke cleanse, burning sage or rosemary, or by putting sun water in a spray bottle and spraying your area with it.

5. For an extra layer of comfort, cast the "Everything Will Be Alright" spell on page 138.

MEDI-TEA-TION BLEND

Mediation and witchcraft often go hand in hand as magic involves a lot of self-reflection, connecting with the universe, and focusing within to find the answers. Unfortunately, it can be hard to find the time or the mindset to practice meditation. We are constantly plugged into other things, our brains never shutting off long enough to let our bodies rest. Instead of finding answers, we feel more lost than ever. Fortunately, this tea can help us settle down and become open to clarity and inner guidance as we meditate. And you'll discover that the more you meditate, the more successful your spells and divination practices will be because you are connecting to your higher power.

1½ teaspoons white tea (*meditation, cleansing, realization, blessings*)

¼ teaspoon ground cardamom (*clarity, wisdom, direction*)

1 teaspoon fresh or dried passionflower (*calming, peace*)

¼ teaspoon cocoa nibs (*spiritual connections, grounding*)

1 cup hot new moon water

INSTRUCTIONS

Put your white tea, cardamom, passionflower, and cocoa nibs into your infuser and place it into your cup. Pour the hot water in and let the tea steep for 3 minutes before stirring the tea three times clockwise. As your tea steeps, get into a comfortable position—sitting cross-legged on the floor, lying down on your bed, sitting outside, or wherever you find it best to meditate. When the tea has finished steeping, drink it quietly, making sure you aren't around anything that could distract you. This time belongs to you and only you. Close your eyes and allow yourself to be still and in the moment and meditate.

FOR A DASH OF MAGIC

🌙 If you have trouble meditating on your own, listen to a meditation playlist or a guided meditation while you drink.

🌙 Hold a piece of clear quartz in your free hand as you sip to help clear your mind.

🌙 The best day to make this tea is during the waning crescent moon, ideal for meditation, or Saturday, which is associated with meditation and breaking bad habits.

SHOW ME THE MONEY

They say money can't buy happiness, but it can certainly help a broke witch from time to time. If you find yourself short on funds or out of a job, or if you just need a little extra in your account to get you through, this blend can help you manifest money quickly, although you should keep your expectations in check. This tea won't help you become a millionaire overnight (unless it makes you suddenly good at picking the lotto numbers), but it may help you get some extra cash when you need it.

---

2 teaspoons green tea (*wealth*)

½ teaspoon fresh or dried thyme
(*prosperity, manifestation, attraction*)

¼ teaspoon ground cinnamon (*wealth, luck, success*)

1 cup hot water

dash of honey (*abundance, manifestation*)

sugar, to taste (*attraction, prosperity, multiplying*)

INSTRUCTIONS

Put the green tea, thyme, and cinnamon in your tea infuser (or loose into your cup if you want to read), and place it into your cup. Pour in the hot water and let it steep for 5 minutes. When the tea is finished steeping, add the honey and sugar and stir clockwise three times. Each time you stir, think about the amount of money you want—for example, "It would be great to have $500 right now," or "My next job will have a $50,000 salary," or something to that effect. Don't say things like "I need this" or "I want money," because you don't want to be desperate for money, and you also want to be exact in how much money you desire—you don't want to be short-changed. When you sip, think about what you would do with that money; visualize it as if it had already happened. Picture it until you have finished drinking.

FOR A DASH OF MAGIC

🌀 Use the "Come to Me" attraction spell on page 136 to make the money you desire come to you faster.

🌀 Draw three dollar signs on a piece of paper and place it under your cup as you drink. This is using sigil magic to get what you want (see page 134 for more on sigil magic).

🌀 Do this spell on a Thursday as it is associated with money spells.

IMMUNI-TEA BOOSTER

Tea, and most herbs in general, have been used to heal people, from a sore throat to a broken heart, for thousands of years. However, if you just don't know what's wrong but you feel a little *blah*, or if you want to prepare for cold and flu season, this is a tea for you. This tea is a strong healing draught that may help cure what ails you and could boost your immunity to protect you from illness. This draught is always very versatile, so you can swap out different ingredients to meet more specific needs (see "For a Dash of Magic" on page 82).

---

1 teaspoon green tea *(rich in antioxidants, boosts metabolism and the immune system, associated with healing and regulating energy)*

1 teaspoon dried elderflower *(boosts the immune system, fights off cold and flu, rich in vitamin C, treats sinus infections, associated with healing, rest, and rebirth)*

½ teaspoon dried calendula petals *(anti-inflammatory, relieves sore throats, rich in antioxidants, associated with healing and protection)*

½ teaspoon ground turmeric *(boosts longevity and the immune system, reduces hay fever symptoms, relieves heartburn, associated with protection and health)*

1 cup hot water

squeeze of fresh orange juice *(rich in vitamin C, associated with healing)*

INSTRUCTIONS

Put the green tea, elderflower, calendula, and turmeric into your infuser and place it into your cup. Pour in the hot water and let it steep for 3 minutes. After it steeps, squeeze in the orange juice and stir three times counterclockwise before drinking. As you sip, imagine a bright, warm light inside your body, healing and protecting you.

FOR A DASH OF MAGIC

If you are dealing with stubborn migraine pain, add ½ teaspoon of peppermint or lavender and leave out the turmeric.

If you are dealing with an upset stomach, switch out the turmeric with ½ teaspoon of lemon balm.

If you are dealing with PMS symptoms and cramps, trade out the turmeric and calendula for a ½ teaspoon of raspberry leaf and a ¼ teaspoon of chamomile.

Brew this with full moon water for an extra dose of healing magic.

Chapter 4

READING YOUR FORTUNE

*T*asseography is an old form of divination that has been practiced for centuries, though it can feel a little intimidating when you're first getting started. However, once you practice, you'll discover how easy the process is, adaptable to any type of tea reading you would like to do. Here is how you do your first tea reading ritual.

GETTING FAMILIAR WITH YOUR CUP

Just like with any magical tool, whether it's a wand, tarot deck, or crystal, it's important to get familiar with your equipment before using it. Obviously, when doing tasseography, one of the most important things you'll need is a teacup. Not a coffee mug or any glassware. A regular old teacup, preferably made from ceramic or porcelain. This is because a teacup has sloping sides that flare out at an angle, so the leaves have an easier time sticking to the sides than they would with the vertical sides of a coffee mug.

Speaking of ease, it's also important to get a cup that is white and blank on the inside. If you have a cup that is too dark on the inside or has too many pictures, it can be harder to see the leaves, especially if you are working with darker tea.

A saucer is also a key element in a tea reading, though if your cup does not come with one, a small plate will work.

When picking out your teacup, you don't have to get fancy; a simple, sturdy white teacup with a strong handle is all you need. You want a cup that you feel comfortable using and that doesn't feel too fragile or delicate in your hand as you'll be moving your cup a lot. Try to use that cup solely for tasseography and other magical practices. You don't want to be drinking your morning tea or coffee and get unsolicited advice!

FOR A DASH OF MAGIC

Place a piece of clear quartz in your teacup when you're not using it. It will cleanse your cup of the energies of the last reading (especially if it was a difficult reading) and keep the magical energies in balance. If you plan on doing a tea reading the next day, place a piece of amethyst in the cup overnight to charge the mug with extra psychic energy.

CHOOSING YOUR TEA

After your teacup, the next most important ingredient in a tasseography is, of course, the tea. While I gave you some tea recipes in Chapter Three, it's essential to stick to simple dark teas for your first few readings as the leaves will be easier for you to see. Here are two teas I recommend:

 LOOSE-LEAF BLACK TEA: Black tea is dark enough to see in your cup without straining your eyes, and it encourages mental clarity and grounding, two things you'll need in a tea reading.

 LOOSE-LEAF OOLONG TEA: Similar to black tea, oolong is a dark-enough color that you can see the tea easily, and its leaves are often longer and thicker than other teas, making it easier to get shapes out of them (and also limiting the possibility of accidentally swallowing the leaves when drinking). Oolong also represents connection, divination, and reflection, giving you a psychic boost as you read. Perfect for beginners.

It's important to use loose-leaf tea for readings and stay away from tea-bag teas found in grocery stores if you can help it. While they are fine for drinking, potions, and spells, they aren't ideal for readings. That's because the tea inside the bags has been processed into finely ground pieces, making them too small to interpret— especially for a beginner.

On the same note, for your first few readings pick a tea that is pleasant for you to drink without any add-ins. Don't add any milk, honey, or sugar, as it can mess up the reading by sticking to the cup or the leaves.

QUESTIONS TO ASK

In the next chapter we will be discussing different types of tea reading rituals for different kind of questions you may have, from as general as "What type of year am I going to have?" to as specific as "What is the name and zodiac sign of my next romantic partner?" But for now, as you start becoming familiar with tea readings, you want to ask specific questions that you can focus on. Asking general questions will typically give you general answers, which aren't very helpful to a beginner. Here are a few sample questions to get you started:

- What is the energy for today?
- What should I focus on today?
- How can I find the right job for me?
- What can I do to bring romance into my life?
- Will I get back together with my ex?
- What should I look for in a partner?
- What do I need to look out for?
- What will help me heal from my grief?
- How can I improve/grow my business?
- What important thing have I forgotten?

These are more specific questions but flexible enough that you won't receive a one-word answer. Remember, tasseography is all about flexibility.

DIVIDING THE CUP

Before beginning your ritual, it's good to divide up your cup into sections. This will make it easier for you when you get to the reading stage as you'll be able to interpret the story better and get a clearer reading. Similar to how you would do card spreads in a tarot card reading, each section has a different meaning. In Chapter Five, we'll be discussing the many ways you can divide up your cup, but for your first reading we will be dividing it into three zones:

- The rim of the cup
- The sides of the cup
- The bottom of the cup

You can use these zones to represent three different things, depending on what type of question you are asking. The first is timing, with the rim representing events happening in the present, the sides representing things that will be happening soon (a few days from now), and the bottom representing the distant future (months from now).

The second is connection, or the physical or symbolic distance between two people. This is good for asking a relationship question. The rim represents something that you have, the sides represent what's farther away, and the bottom represents what's very far away.

Lastly, the zones can be used to represent the intensity of the future. The rim represents a life-changing event. The sides represent some shake-ups, and the bottom represents things you don't have to worry about.

If dividing up zones sounds a little overwhelming to you, especially for your first reading, the simplest way to divide a cup is by past and future. Use the handle of the cup to divide the cup into two halves: the left and the right. Whatever symbols appear on the left side of the cup represent the past, while the symbols on the right represent the future. Whatever lands near the handle represents the present.

ABOUT THE HANDLE: In tasseography, the handle of the cup represents the energy conduit that connects our physical realm with the spiritual one. Think of it as kind of like a magic wand, linking you and the magic together. In a reading, the handle represents you, the reader, and the handle is what guides the reading and how you look at your cup. When leaves land near your handle, it usually relates to your immediate surroundings or what will have the greatest effect on you, so keep that in mind as you read.

THE RITUAL

Now for the moment you've all been waiting for (unless you skipped ahead to this section), it's time to get to the ritual. Like most things in witchcraft, how you do your tasseography ritual is fluid and flexible, customizable for any witch. However, for your first time, I'll walk you through it step by step. When you get more comfortable in your practice, feel free to add the teas, rituals, and spells found in Chapters Three, Five, and Six or add your magic to it.

SETTING: Tasseography can be done at any time and in any place, though for your first few readings, you may want to find a nice quiet place with good lighting, free of distraction. Most people prefer to read at a table where they can keep their feet firmly on the ground and keep their cup and saucer steady. Traditionally, tea readings were done in the morning, but the exact time you do a reading isn't important. What's important is how much time you give yourself to read. You don't want to rush yourself or do a reading when you have a lot going on as this will take time, especially when you're a beginner. This should be a quiet, calming, and reflective time. So, find a nice, comfortable place to sit, and light a few candles or incense to add a witchy, calming vibe.

---

teacup and saucer

1 tablespoon loose-leaf tea

1 cup hot water

paper and pencil *(or your phone) to record your results*

this book

STEP 1: Once you've gathered all your materials together and found a comfortable, quiet spot, close your eyes and take a few calming breaths to ground yourself. Some people even meditate before reading to get better connected to the spiritual realm and open up their intuition. It can also calm you if you're nervous. Grounding is always important in any fortune-telling practice. Remember: never divine when you're nervous—it never goes well.

STEP 2: Once you're grounded, place your tea leaves into your cup and pour the hot water in.

STEP 3: As you wait for your tea to cool, hold the cup in your hands and close your eyes. Visualize transferring your energy into the cup.

STEP 4: Think about your question, and even ask it aloud to the cup.

STEP 5: Sip your tea while thinking about your question. Put your mouth tightly to the rim of the cup as you sip to reduce the number of leaves that you swallow.

> **MAGIC TRICK:** If you cannot handle your tea leaves being loose in your cup or just don't enjoy drinking it with all the leaves, get a tea infuser with very large holes so most of the tea escapes. You may not get a perfect reading, but enough tea will fall out to give you a pretty good reading without the sensory issues.

STEP 6: When there is only a sip of tea left (about a tablespoon), hold the cup in your left hand (the hand of intuition) and swirl the liquid three times, clockwise. Remember to do it very gently so you don't splash the tea on yourself.

STEP 7: Still using your left hand, slowly turn the cup upside down on the saucer. Leave it there for about a minute or so to drain. Tap the bottom of the cup with your knuckle three times to loosen the leaves.

STEP 8: Rotate the cup three times. Then, using your dominant hand, turn the cup upright, placing the handle pointed toward you.

STEP 9: Get ready to read!

THE READING

When I did my first tea reading, my automatic reaction when I flipped over my cup for the first time was: "Oh no, I did something wrong! This doesn't look like anything!" and I panicked. As it turns out, this is the normal reaction to a tea reading. Unlike some other forms of fortune-telling, like tarot, which has clear rules and meanings for each card, tea readings rely more on your own intuition and interpretation. So don't panic if the first thing you see when you turn over your cup is a bunch of leaves—it's going to take a minute. Your tasseography message isn't going to be spelled out clearly for you in actual letters. If it does, then you'd better break out the sage, witch, because you got ghosts.

The best thing to do is let your mind wander as you're looking. Don't hyper-focus on any particular area. Let images jump out at you when they're ready. Start out by looking at the largest symbol first and making your way down to the smallest. And make sure you rotate your cup during your reading so you can look at your leaves from different angles; that will help you see different symbols and shapes. The number of shapes you see in your cup is usually an indicator of what's going on in your life. If you see a lot of symbols in your cup, you may have many life-changing events going on.

When you start seeing symbols in your teacup, write them down immediately, going on your first impressions. Don't overanalyze it; don't stress out over whether that weird line on the rim is an *S* or a snake. If you thought "snake" as soon as you looked at it, then it's a snake. Often, our first impression is our intuition at work.

As you write stuff down, take note of what and where everything is. For example, you may write down something like this: "Snake on the rim, boat at the handle, broken heart at the bottom." If you have divided your cup into three zones, mark that down as well. "Snake on the rim—the present; boat at the handle—near future; broken heart at the bottom—distant future." And so on.

Once you have everything written down, and you can't see anything else in your cup, it's time to tell your story! One of the most magical aspects of tea reading is that you are able to use what you find in your teacup to tell yourself a story about the future.

Next, take a look at the symbols and the placements you wrote down and start to decode them. You can turn to the Symbol Dictionary to help you out, but don't discount your own associations for things. For example, if you have a boat on the side of your cup, traditionally, it means someone is traveling to see you. However, if you own a boat or live near the water where a lot of boats come in, the symbol could have a different meaning for you. So, keep that in mind.

Once you have decoded everything, look at what you deciphered and try to figure out what story is being told. Here's a demonstration using the example I have given above:

Snake (worry and anxiety) on the rim, boat (friend traveling to visit) on the side, broken heart (heartbreak) on the bottom.

This story can go in a few different directions:

 If you divided the zones by time, it could mean you are very worried about your friend who is coming to visit you in the next few days. This visit may not go well, and in the next couple of months you may have a falling-out and your friendship could be over. Or you had a falling-out with a friend, which made you nervous and upset, and now they are coming to see you.

 If you divided the zones by connection, it could mean that you are constantly anxious in a relationship, and someone (maybe a false friend or someone who should not be trusted) is keeping you apart. You may need to have space between you and your partner to avoid heartbreak.

If you divided up your zones by intensity, you might be anxious over a major life change that is giving you stress. You may be moving across the sea in a couple of months. However, you shouldn't be worried because it's all going to end well, and you will move on from your current heartbreak.

Because tea readings are so personal, the possibilities are endless. Trust your gut as you write your story, and, once again, don't overthink it!

FOR A DASH OF MAGIC

As you grow in your tea reading abilities, it's very important to keep a tasseography journal, making an entry of each one of your readings. You can use a regular notebook or a bullet journal, or even just keep one on your computer or phone. Take a picture of your cup; write down your question, what you saw, and your initial prediction; and record what ultimately ended up happening. Not only will this help you keep track of how good (or bad) your accuracy was, but it will also document your growth as a reader.

THE MAGIC WORDS

The best advice I can give to first-time readers is these magic words:

You don't have to be perfect at this.

This is good witchcraft advice, and also just good life advice in general. As a type-A Virgo sun, I understand the drive for perfection and the near obsession to be excellent at something on the first try. When I first got into divination, it was really hard for me because

I was so scared of being wrong or not being "good" at it. But you don't have to be perfect at this! You don't have to be good on your first try or your hundredth try. What's important is that you keep listening to your intuition, and you keep practicing. Being hard on yourself isn't going to make you a better reader, a better witch, or even a better person. It's just going to make you stressed, anxious, and unhappy. Just keep showing up with an open mind and keep trying, simply because you enjoy doing it. Remember, practice makes magic!

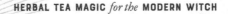

Chapter 5

SPILLING THE TEA: TEA LEAF RITUALS

*N*ow that we've covered the basics of a tea reading, it's time to play around a little with your craft. Here are a few tea reading rituals to help guide you in any situation you may have.

THE DAILY FORECAST

This is a quick and easy tea reading for the start of your morning. This ritual is great for when you want to look at what's up ahead for your day and decide how to best prepare. Make sure you have at least thirty minutes to spare to do this ritual. If you rush, you could "spill your tea" on yourself, and not in a fun way.

---·❖·---

teacup

saucer or small plate

tea *(see tea blend recommendations in the "For a Dash of Magic" section below)*

your cell phone

some breakfast *(it's the most important meal of the day)*

---·❖·---

THE RITUAL

STEP 1: While you're waiting for your water to heat up, take your cup in your dominant hand and look into it. Visualize the face of a clock with the handle representing 12 and space for 1, 2, 3, 4, and so on. If you're having a hard time visualizing, use this graph as a guide:

HERBAL TEA MAGIC *for the* **MODERN WITCH**

This represents the hours in the day. You can also change it so it's in line with your schedule. For example, if your day starts at 9 a.m., put the 9 at the handle.

STEP 2: Prepare your loose-leaf tea as you usually would. Pour the hot water in.

STEP 3: While the tea steeps, place your phone next to the cup. This will help charge up the tea and bring it more in tune with your day, especially if you have your calendar app, email, or to-do list up.

STEP 4: Make breakfast while the tea steeps.

STEP 5: When your tea is ready, gaze into the cup and visualize the best possible version of your day (e.g., completing what you need to get done, the best possible outcomes for specific events of your day, etc.). If you want to perform a spell (see suggested spells in the "For a Dash of Magic" section below), now is the time.

STEP 6: Sip your tea, eat your breakfast, and mentally prepare for the day as you normally do (checking your email, studying, watching the news, getting ready, scrolling through social media, etc.).

STEP 7: When you only have a little tea left in your cup, tip it over onto your saucer and wait a minute. Then flip it back to reveal your reading.

STEP 8: Do your tea reading, making notes on what you see. If the leaves are close to the top (rim) of the cup, that means the event will happen in the a.m. hours. If the leaves are near the bottom of the cup, the event will occur in the p.m. hours.

EXAMPLE: If you see a dog at the top of the 9 section of your cup and an anchor near the bottom of your 3 section, the dog event will happen at 9 a.m., while the anchor event will happen at 3 p.m. (To see what dog and anchor symbolize, check the Symbol Dictionary at the end of the book.)

TIP: If you are a commuter, snap a photo of your reading on your phone and decode the message on your ride to work.

STEP 9: When you finish your reading, clean up and start your day. If you see any interesting events, make a note on your calendar (for example, "at 10 a.m., mild delays are predicted"). It's a great way to see how accurate your reading skills are and to remind you of your predictions. At the end of the day, check back on your reading and see how much has come to pass.

FOR A DASH OF MAGIC

- While you can use just about any type of tea for this, try "Good-Thyme Tea" (page 53), "The Midas Blend" (page 55), or "Anti Anxie-tea" (page 51), depending on your needs.

- Perform the "Good Vibes Only" spell on page 141 to ensure your day is a good one.

- Once a week, go back and look at how many of your daily forecast predictions came true. This will help you read symbols better and learn how to read and understand your intuition.

IT'S JUST A PHASE: A LUNAR CALENDAR READING

The moon has always played an essential role in our lives here on Earth. It controls the tides of our oceans, the behaviors of certain animals, and the stability of our seasons. For centuries people used the lunar cycle to track their menstrual cycles as both last the same amount of time (29.5 days). Astrologers keep track of the moon and what sign it's in to make predictions.

Witches have also always been invested in the moon. Pagans and Wiccans worship moon deities and the moon's power in their spells and rituals. Every phase of the moon, from the darkness of the new moon to the last sliver of the waning crescent, holds its own power and meaning. Here is a brief overview of what each phase of the lunar cycle represents:

- **NEW MOON:** New beginnings, setting intentions, new projects, planting seeds to watch them grow.
- **WAXING CRESCENT:** Foundation, grounding, taking the first solid steps toward your goals. Good time for manifesting.
- **FIRST QUARTER:** Connection, networking, sharing with others. Time of potential challenges and change.
- **WAXING GIBBOUS:** Preparation, incoming abundance, building momentum, creating realistic plans for the future.
- **FULL MOON:** The search for peace, things manifesting, releasing negativity. This is the highest power and highest energy.

WANING GIBBOUS: Reflection and an awakening of sorts. Opportunities for analysis and ideal for showing gratitude.

 THIRD QUARTER: Release and letting go of things that no longer serve us.

WANING CRESCENT: Emotions, self-care, and the feeling of feels. The need for rest and recharging.

You can also use the lunar phases to make predictions, especially if you use astrology. Combine moon magic and tasseography together to see what's coming up during the next lunar cycle so you can plan ahead.

---

cup and saucer

tea

a calendar (*preferably a lunar calendar, which can be purchased as a paper planner or found on a phone app, but any calendar will work*)

pen and paper

THE RITUAL

The best day to do this reading is right before the next new moon so you can look at the cycle fully. Do this reading at night for the best results.

STEP 1: Plot the lunar cycle on your calendar if you're not using a lunar calendar. Make a note of what astrology signs the moon phases will be in during this period. For example, the new moon in Aries, the full moon in Scorpio, etc. This information can be found on your lunar calendar or via a quick web search. The astrological information will be important when you do your full reading, especially if you're interested in astrology.

STEP 2: Divide the cup into eight sections from new moon to waning crescent, with the full moon at the handle, like so:

STEP 3: Pour your loose-leaf tea into the cup and add water.

STEP 4: As your tea steeps, look into your cup and visualize the month ahead. What events do you have coming up? What do you want to happen? Visualize as you stir your tea three times, clockwise.

STEP 5: Drink your tea. When you only have a little tea left in your cup, tip it over onto your saucer and wait a minute. Then flip it back to reveal your reading.

STEP 6: Do your reading and make notes on what you see.

EXAMPLE: You see an acorn at the top part of your cup in the new moon section. That can mean you are starting a new project or a new phase in a relationship. The upcoming new moon will be in Aries, so this new beginning could be happening very quickly! Meanwhile, if you see a lighthouse near the bottom of the third quarter moon section, you may have to get rid of friends who aren't helping you.

STEP 7: Keep track of the lunar cycle and your prediction to see if what you read in your cup came to pass.

FOR A DASH OF MAGIC

- If you want to add some more lunar magic, brew your tea using water that's been charged by the moon (see page 48 for information on making moon water).

- Use oolong tea for this ritual as it is associated with the moon.

- Set calendar alerts on your phone based on your predictions to give yourself a little heads-up (in case you forget about your predictions).

THE YEAR AHEAD

We've talked about using tea readings to predict the day ahead and the month ahead; now let's talk about using a reading to look into the year ahead. This ritual can be done at any time of the year, but it's ideal when starting a new year. This could be the start of the calendar year (January), the Chinese New Year (February), the astrological new year (April 20), or even your birthday. Whatever date you choose, just make sure you only do it once a year. Unlike the daily and lunar readings, doing a yearly reading multiple times a year can get really confusing, and your cup may get frustrated with you.

cup and saucer

tea

your grimoire

a calendar *(optional)*

THE RITUAL

STEP 1: Grab your cup and saucer, tea, grimoire, and calendar, and find a quiet place to do your reading without any distractions.

STEP 2: Mentally divide your cup into twelve sections, one for each month, with your current month located at the handle, like this:

STEP 3: Brew your tea and sip. As you drink, visualize the year ahead, and what you would like to happen in the upcoming year. You can also customize this reading with a more specific question (for example, "What will my career look like this year?" "What will my love life look like this year?" "What will my health look like this year?").

STEP 4: When there is only half a swallow left, hold the cup in your left hand and swirl the liquid three times, clockwise. Slowly turn the cup upside down on the saucer. Leave it there for about a minute to drain. As it drains, think about your question one last time.

STEP 5: Flip over your cup and start your reading. To help organize your reading, create twelve different sections in your grimoire, one for each month, and write down what you see in that section of the cup. For example, if you see a bird, a heart, and a tree in the April section of the cup, you will write those observations in the April section of the grimoire.

As you go through your reading, pay special attention to any number you see. For example, if you see a five in the "June" section of your cup, mark it down. It might be an important day. You can also put alerts on your calendar app for a reminder.

STEP 6: Keep notes on your reading to use later, especially at the end of each month, to reflect on what came to pass.

FOR A DASH OF MAGIC

🌙 Do a lunar calendar reading (page 99) and compare those notes to the ones you took for that specific month in your "The Year Ahead" reading. What is consistent? What is different? This will give you a fuller picture of the month ahead.

🌙 If you have any trouble understanding what may happen in a certain month, or if you would like more clarity, pull a tarot card.

🌙 Use the "Third Eye Opener" tea blend on page 57 for this ritual as you'll need a strong third eye to look that far ahead into the future.

SEASONS CHANGE AND SO DO I: A RITUAL FOR SEEING WHAT EACH SEASON MAY HOLD

Paying attention to the changing of the season is an important part of herbal magic, as certain herbs have growing and harvesting seasons. Like tea, some herbs have a special correlation to a particular season. So, it only makes sense to keep the seasons in mind when creating potions and performing spells to learn what is up ahead. This tea ritual will help you gain insight into what may happen during the next four seasons of your life: winter, spring, summer, and fall. This is great to get insight on what's ahead—and perfect for beginners who may find "The Year Ahead" ritual a little overwhelming.

cup and saucer

tea

pen and paper

THE RITUAL

STEP 1: While you're waiting for your water to heat up, take your cup in your dominant hand and look into it. Mentally (or on a piece of paper if you have trouble visualizing) divide the cup into four sections, with each section representing a season. Like this:

It doesn't matter where you put each season, but make sure the current season is the section where the handle is. So, if it's June, label the handle "summer," then go clockwise with the rest of the seasons: fall, winter, spring.

STEP 2: Place your loose-leaf tea into your cup and pour the water in. Drink.

STEP 3: When there is a little less than a swallow of tea left, do your regular tea leaf ritual.

STEP 4: Do your reading, writing down what you see in each section. Take your time with these, and even take a picture if you want to look at it later.

STEP 5: Go over your notes and create a story of what may happen according to the reading. For example, if you see a sword in your summer section, a bridge in fall, and a butterfly in summer, it may mean that you will gain some authority (like getting a promotion) in the summer, then achieve more career success in the fall, before going through a rebirth period in the winter.

STEP 6: Save your reading to look back on it later during each season. Pay attention to how much tea is where. If you see a lot of leaves in the spring section, you may have a hectic spring. If you don't see anything in the winter section, it may be a very quiet season.

FOR A DASH OF MAGIC

If you're doing your reading during a particular season, pick a tea or herbal blend representing that season. Make the "Basic Witch Brew" (page 66) for fall, a peppermint-infused tea for winter, floral teas for spring, and the "Good-Thyme Tea" (page 53) for summer.

If you want a more in-depth reading about a specific season, do a second tea reading with the cup divided into three sections representing the three months in that season.

WHO IS MY NEXT LOVER?

Could your next relationship be found at the bottom of your teacup? When we talk about tasseography, it's usually in the context of timing or events, but tea readings can also be used to predict our next relationships as well. For this ritual, you will use the leaves to learn all about the next lover who will be entering your life. While we'll be using the term "lover," you can use this reading for various relationships: soulmate, twin flame, spouse, best friend, business partner, or even predicting your future children. At its core, this reading is intended to discover the traits, personality, and basic information of a significant person coming into your life.

---

cup and saucer

"Love Potion No. 9" tea *(page 59)*

pen and paper

rose quartz

THE RITUAL

STEP 1: Before you begin, write down a short list of the information you're hoping to gain from this reading. For example, you could use this reading to discover your future lover's initials, their possible age or birthday, occupation, and general personality traits. Try not to get too specific about the information; you aren't going to find your lover's name, social security number, and blood type at the bottom of your cup—though I would be really impressed if you did. This list is just to help you when you get to the reading stage, so you know what to look for.

STEP 2: Make your "Love Potion No. 9" tea (or just prepare regular oolong tea).

STEP 3: Drink your brew. As you sip, hold the rose quartz in your hand and visualize your perfect lover. What would you like out of your next relationship? What are you looking for?

STEP 4: When there is only half a swallow left, hold the cup in your left hand and swirl the liquid three times, clockwise. Slowly turn the cup upside down on the saucer. Leave it there for about a minute or so to drain.

STEP 5: Before you flip the cup over, say three times (either out loud or in your mind), "Reveal my lover to me," tapping the cup three times with your ring finger.

STEP 6: Flip your cup over and take a look at what's inside. As you write down your observations, keep these particular aspects in mind:

- Any letter or number. (Letters can represent your lover's initials, while numbers can represent their age, birthday, or even when you'll meet)

- The location of the leaves. (If you see a lot of leaves on the top of the cup, you'll meet your lover very soon, but it may be a surface-level relationship. If you see a lot of leaves near the bottom, you may not meet your lover for a long time, but it will be a very intense relationship. Many leaves near the handle means that you will be remarkably close to your lover and they will be a big part of your life.)

Remember to write down everything you see and to take photos to look at later (especially when you meet your next lover).

STEP 7: When you're doing your interpretation to make a prediction, remember to be flexible and even write down multiple interpretations. For example, if you see in your cup the letter A, the numbers 2 and 6 next to each other, a ring, a boat, and a coin, this could manifest in a few different ways:

 You'll meet someone whose first name starts with the letter A, who is 26 years old, and who is traveling in a different country. This is the person you will marry.

 You'll meet someone on February 6 on a business trip overseas. You will think this person is great until you learn that they are married and you are in the middle of an affair. (Scandal!)

 Your future spouse's last name starts with an A, and they work with boats for a living. You will be married to them on the 26th.

Play around with your prediction and listen to your intuition. If you feel drawn to a certain interpretation, go with it. Save these in your grimoire for later.

FOR A DASH OF MAGIC

 If you'd like to learn the birth chart of your future lover, do the "Zodiac Wheel Reading" on page 172. If you want to know when you'll meet them, do "The Year Ahead" reading on page 103 or the "Seasons Change and So Do I" ritual on page 106 with that question in mind to get a better answer.

 The best day to do this ritual is Friday as it is ruled by the planet Venus, making it an ideal time for love magic.

🌙 If you are interested in working with color magic, use a red or pink cup (though still white on the inside) to do this ritual as red and pink are associated with love.

🌙 If you want to meet your love quicker, perform the "Come to Me" spell on page 136 while brewing another cup of "Love Potion No. 9" (it doesn't need to be loose this time), with your reading predictions in front of you.

🌙 For an extra boost, write a love sigil on the bottom of the cup (see page 134 for more information on sigil magic).

A NOTE ON CONSENT: As mentioned in the "Love Potion No. 9" recipe on page 59, consent is essential when it comes to magic, which means that casting spells that force people to fall in love with someone against their will is a hard "no." Do not use the information found in your reading as an excuse to use a love spell or make someone fall in love with you. For example, say that you do a reading and, from your interpretation, determine that your next lover will be Reese, a person you already have a crush on. While you're excited, you remember that Reese just entered a new relationship with someone else. This does not give you permission to attempt a love spell or spoil Reese's new relationship because you "are meant for each other." Remember: what's meant for you will come to you.

THE DISTANCE
BETWEEN US

Sometimes relationships just don't work out the way you plan them. Maybe your romantic partner has been picking fights with you almost daily. Perhaps you and a friend haven't talked in ages and don't know how to make things right again. A sibling rivalry has gotten out of control. Whatever the situation may be, if you are having trouble in your relationships and need to get a new perspective, try looking at the bottom of your teacup.

———————— ❃ ————————

cup and saucer

tea

your grimoire

a device that plays music

———————— ❃ ————————

THE RITUAL

STEP 1: Make a playlist about the person you currently feel distant from. It could be songs that remind you of them or the good times you had together, songs that have meaning in your relationship, songs that remind you of the fight you had, or songs that represent the distance in your current relationship. Music is a form of magic that connects people to different emotions, feelings, places, and times. In situations where we do not have the words to say what we feel, music can help connect you to those feelings.

STEP 2: Gather the rest of your supplies, if you haven't already, and prepare your tea.

STEP 3: Start your playlist and sip your tea. As you drink, think about the other person you are having issues with. If you can, replay the last conversation you had in your head; how did it make you feel? Write your feelings down if you wish, but continue to think about them as you drink; think about the good times as well as the bad.

STEP 4: When there is only half a swallow left, hold the cup in your left hand and swirl the liquid three times, clockwise. Turn the cup upside down on the saucer. Leave it there for about a minute or so to drain.

STEP 5: Flip the cup over and look inside. Pay attention to these four places:

 THE RIM: This represents the fight on the surface or how deep the distance is. If there are a lot of leaves, the fight wasn't that deep, just a heat-of-the-moment argument. If you don't see much here, the fight was much more intense and will not be easy to fix. Symbols found here will tell you more about the fight or why you're now distant.

THE MIDDLE/SIDES: The leaves found here represent the divide between you two beyond the surface level. These are the hidden factors of the relationship and things that you may not be aware of.

 THE BOTTOM: This represents what you could do to mend the relationship and what you can expect going forward. If you see nothing on the bottom of the cup and most of the leaves at the top, the distance will be resolved quickly. If there's nothing on the bottom and most of the leaves are on the side, this relationship may never be healed.

THE HANDLE: This represents your part in the fight and your feelings about it. When you hold the cup out by the handle, check the spot exactly across from the handle; that section represents the other person's part in the rift and their feelings.

STEP 6: Write down all your observations and predictions in your grimoire.

STEP 7: Use what you have learned to move forward.

FOR A DASH OF MAGIC

 If you want an extra boost in mending the relationship, perform the "Sweeten Your Words" spell on page 144 or the "Getting Out of Hot Water" spell on page 150. Or, if you're hoping to move on from this relationship, try the "Let Go and Let Grow" spell on page 158.

Or if spell crafting isn't your thing yet, use music! Create a playlist full of making-up/getting-back-together/happy songs. Then start singing them as loud as you can—no matter what type of singer you are. Dance to it as well. Singing and dancing create energy and voice your desires, thus creating magic. If you want to move on from this relationship, do the same thing, only with a playlist of breakup/moving-on songs.

If the person you are having a problem with has a favorite tea, use that to represent them.

SHOULD I BE WORRIED? A RITUAL TO FIND OUT WHEN YOU NEED TO PANIC

There's an old saying that you should always expect the unexpected. However, when you live in a world where it feels like *anything* can happen, you may feel like you have to worry about *everything* all the time, which can be very stressful. So, this is a ritual for all you overthinking and anxious witches who just need to know what crisis they should be worrying about. This is a great tea to have when you feel overwhelmed, nervous, or just need to know what to worry about. I know you because I am one of you.

---

cup and saucer

tea

grimoire

a separate piece of paper to write on

a candle *(optional)*

THE RITUAL

STEP 1: Get your cup and saucer and begin to prepare your tea.

STEP 2: As you sip your tea, write out a list of everything that is troubling you on a separate piece of paper—from big issues like money or relationships, to small things like "My friend said 'Hi' to me in a different tone, I think she hates me," or "My crush didn't like my selfie, what does that mean?" Don't judge yourself for these thoughts; don't call them silly or tell yourself other people have it worse. Just write it all down.

STEP 3: When there is only half a swallow left, hold the cup in your left hand and swirl the liquid three times, clockwise. Turn the cup upside down on the saucer. Leave it there for about a minute or so to drain.

STEP 4: Flip your cup over and look inside. Pay attention to these key areas:

THE RIM: This is the stuff you have to worry about. What you see on the rim represents major concerns you need to address or get ready for. It can also represent dramatic changes that are coming into your life. So, yes, you should worry about this.

THE MIDDLE/SIDES: Leaves here represent some minor shake-ups that could become problems at some point but are not problems at this moment. That doesn't mean that you should ignore what you see here, but it's a good indication of what you should be looking out for in the future to see if you can prevent these shake-ups before they happen.

THE BOTTOM: The leaves and symbols you see at the bottom represent things you don't have to worry about. These are non-issues. So, if you've been worried about work, your health, or your relationships and you see them at the bottom of your cup, you have nothing to worry about. Breathe a sigh of relief if you see a lot of leaves at the bottom of your cup.

STEP 5: Record your reading and observations in your grimoire.

STEP 6: Light your candle.

STEP 7: Take your piece of paper where you have written all of your worries, and, using your fire-safety skills, burn the piece of paper with your candle. As you watch the paper burn, visualize all of your fears being burned away and out of your life. Alternatively, you can also destroy the paper by ripping it up and throwing it away or putting it in a shredder.

FOR A DASH OF MAGIC

- Use the "Anti Anxie-tea" blend on page 51 or the "Negative Thought Repellent" blend on page 62 if you need a little extra anxiety relief or calming down.

- If you still feel anxious after performing this reading (especially if you get some bad news), do the "Everything Will Be Alright" spell on page 138.

- If you feel you need some extra protection, put some thyme or lavender or an amethyst crystal by your window and doors to protect your home.

WHERE AM I GOING? A TEA RITUAL FOR FINDING DIRECTION

As we go along through life's journey, we sometimes get lost on our path. Our internal compass goes out of sync, and we become directionless, unable to decide where to go next. It can be a scary and overwhelming time, and it's usually after a major life change: graduating from school, losing a job, the aftermath of a breakup, surviving a terrible experience. These feelings can also arise after feeling stuck in a rut for too long. When you are feeling lost, it's time to access your spiritual compass in the form of your teacup. Do this ritual to read what direction your life is going in—and what you should do about it. This reading is great for beginners because you are mainly focusing on what direction the leaves are in to get your answer. Though finding and analysis in the symbols you see are encouraged; they are not the most important thing this time.

---·❄·---

cup and saucer

tea

grimoire

spoon

---·❄·---

THE RITUAL

STEP 1: Take your cup in your dominant hand and look at it. Mentally and visually, divide the cup into four sections: north, south, east, and west. Make the handle north and label the rest as such, like this:

STEP 2: Prepare your tea. With your spoon, stir your drink three times clockwise, starting at the north point. If you have a specific question about where you are going (like "Where am I going in my career?" or "Where am I going in my love life?"), ask it now.

STEP 3: Drink your tea. As you sip, visualize yourself walking down a path; this is a very clear path that is easy to follow. As you continue to walk (and drink), the path becomes more winding and harder to see. As you finish your tea, visualize the path disappearing, and you are left standing before a compass. What direction is the arrow pointing you toward?

STEP 4: When there is only half a swallow left, hold the cup in your left hand and swirl the tea three times, clockwise. Turn the cup upside down on the saucer. Leave it there for about a minute or so to drain.

STEP 5: Flip your cup over and look inside. When you set the cup down to read, place the handle away from you. Take a look at where most of the leaves are located.

If most of the leaves are scattered to the north (the handle): In witchcraft, north represents the physical body (which is why it's located at the handle). It also represents health issues, potential health issues, and healing the body. This is one of the most powerful directions because, while its ruling element is earth, it also deals with the spiritual plane and the increase of intuition. We are rising upon the physical realm and into the spiritual.

If your leaves are pointing north, it means you are currently in a state of healing, whether you are recovering from health issues or your body is dealing with a physical change. However, you are on the healing path now. Trust your intuition now and follow it. Ask for guidance.

If most of the leaves are scattered to the east: East represents new beginnings and a time of great change. East deals with career issues, strength, clarity, and new business opportunities. Corresponding with the air element, east deals with our financial security and financial future. Associated with the mind, east gives us extra energy, can heal the mind, and can transmit information.

If your leaves point you east, it means that you may be going through a major change in your career or dealing with money issues. You may be in between jobs at the moment or stressed about money. However, this is a very positive direction because things are going to be changing for you. A new beginning is on the horizon, and life is going to change for the better. Focus on new goals, research your career, and take care of your mind.

If most of the leaves are scattered to the south: South represents challenges and hardships that you have already endured or will have to endure in the future. But don't panic! It's not all doom and gloom. South, associated with the fire element, is also deeply creative, associated with relationships, love, emotions, and artistic pursuits.

If your leaves point you south, you may be having relationship or emotional issues. If you are a creative person and get this direction, you may have been suffering from a period of creative block, but that period will soon be over. To heal from your issues, you are going to need some serious willpower. Work through this challenge using art and creativity. Tap into your emotions to find your way again.

If most of the leaves are scattered to the west: West represents endings and forgiveness. West, associated with water, encourages us to let go and move on. It also deals with self-esteem, self-worth, forgiveness (of both yourself and others), cleansing, and unconditional love. West can represent a very emotional period because sometimes endings are deeply sad, but sometimes you have to move on to be renewed.

If your leaves point you west, it means there may be some endings in your future. Things that haven't been working in a long time or that have made you feel bad about yourself are finally exiting your life. While this may be a bittersweet ending, it is ultimately for the best and leading you to your highest good. To find direction again, practice forgiveness.

If the leaves are located in two different places: If you have some leaves scattered in multiple directions, you may be at a fork in the road where you need to choose between two life paths. For example, say you feel listless in your life and wonder if moving across the country and starting over is the right idea. Some of the tea leaves are in the east, and some are in the south. East represents moving cross-country, where you will have new opportunities and find the right career path for you. South represents staying where you are, where you may face more challenges but will find creative ways to deal with them and even find love. Use the symbols in your cup for clues.

 If the leaves are scattered in all directions: Wow! You are really lost, huh? Don't worry! It's going to be okay. This can mean that you are being pulled in multiple directions in different areas of your life. Look for symbols in each section of your cup for clues.

STEP 6: Record your reading in your grimoire to save for later.

FOR A DASH OF MAGIC

 If you are pulled in two directions, use a deck of tarot cards or a pendulum to ask for clarification.

 To get pulled toward the right direction quicker, use the "Come to Me" spell on page 136 with the intention of finding your path.

 Incorporate the direction that you have been given into your magic practices. For example, if you get north, brew the "Immuni-tea Booster" on page 81 and drink it while facing north. If you get east, place career-boosting crystals on the east side of your room.

REVEAL YOURSELF! A RITUAL FOR GETTING TO THE TRUTH

Part of the reason why we do divination is to get to the bottom of issues—to uncover truths that lurk deep below the surface, often clouded by deceit or our own limited understanding of the situation. While we are meant to trust our intuition, sometimes we need a little help to find the truth. This tea reading ritual is intended to help you uncover the truth to certain questions you may have. It can also be used to help reveal your own feelings that you may be hiding from yourself. The goal here is to help you gain clarity, increase your intuition, and get to the bottom of things.

cup and saucer

tea

grimoire

a separate sheet of paper

spoon

THE RITUAL

STEP 1: Gather your supplies and sit in front of them. Take a moment to close your eyes and ground yourself. Focus on being present in this moment. You are going to need to be very in tune with yourself for this reading.

STEP 2: Prepare your tea as normal.

STEP 3: As you wait for your tea to cool, write down the question or concern you wish to get to the bottom of. What do you want to be revealed? This question can about anything, from what the human resources person thought about your job interview, to wondering if your feelings for your longtime friend are actually romantic. Make notes under the question, writing down any important details: dates, people, facts, and your feelings about the situation. What vibes is it giving off? Write it all down.

STEP 4: When your tea has cooled enough to sip, take your spoon and stir your tea three times. With each stir, say, "Reveal your secrets to me. Tell me what I need to know for my highest good."

STEP 5: Sip your tea, still thinking about your situation. Take additional notes as they come.

STEP 6: When there is only half a swallow left, hold the cup in your left hand and swirl the tea three times, clockwise. Turn the cup upside down on the saucer. Let the rest of the tea drain for about a minute.

STEP 7: Flip your cup over and look inside. Write down everything you see, every symbol that comes to mind. Trust your gut and don't overthink your answers. When you have everything written, go over the question you wrote down and see which symbols you got tie into the question you asked. What has been revealed?

FOR A DASH OF MAGIC

- Use the "Third Eye Opener" blend on page 57 to get more clarity in your reading.
- Perform this reading during a full moon, using the moon's full brightness to reveal what has been hidden.

Perform the "Getting Out of Hot Water" spell on page 150 if you are using the reading to find a way to get out of a difficult situation.

A NOTE: Just a reminder that just because you revealed something in your cup does not mean you should use this reading as evidence to confront someone. If you use this reading to see if your partner is cheating on you, and you get a reading that says that they are, do not confront them, fight with them, or break up with them, just because your teacup told you to. Talk it out first!

Chapter 6

SPELL IT OUT: TEA SPELLS FOR AN ENCHANTED BREW

Spells may be the thing you're most familiar with when it comes to magic, but it may also be the thing about magic that intimates you the most. You've probably seen spells done numerous times in various forms of media: from made-up Latin phrases to long rhyming poems that sometimes backfire on the main character. But what is a spell in real life?

Well, more likely than not, you've probably seen spells being performed in your daily life. You may even have performed a few yourself without realizing it.

A spell, at its essence, is a series of words that are performed with magical intention to be manifested into powerful energy and action. Being a writer and a witch, I am all too familiar with the power of words and what they can create. However, you don't need to be a writer to experience the power of words—you feel it almost every day of your life, often in mundane ways. Giving yourself a pep talk right before giving a presentation, singing along to the car radio, memorizing every lyric. You probably remember the hurtful words someone said about you, just as you felt the power of telling someone "no" and them listening. These are all examples of the power of words.

You've probably heard the phrase "thoughts become reality"—in most cases, they really do. If you worry about something bad happening to you, that bad thing is more likely to occur because it has become all you can think and talk about. Similarly, when you think, talk, and act like everything will work out for you, it's more likely that things will work out for you. While life is never black and white, and sometimes you will feel negative, depressed, and angry (and for justifiable reasons), it's important to look outside those feelings to get clarity. If you continue to live inside your own bubble of negative talk, you'll never leave.

Words have power because we have power. There are a million cheesy witch metaphors I can use here: we are all made of cosmos and stars, magic runs through our veins, we are the grandchildren of the witches they didn't burn, and all that jazz. However, we have power simply because we are alive. We are alive to create and expel energy, to interact with others, to make things, to think, to dream. We are alive, and therefore we are magical. And, just as plants make brews magical, we make words magical.

So, if you're feeling a little nervous about spell casting, don't worry; spells only work if you are adding energy to them. They aren't going to blow up in your face because you said a word wrong or the spell didn't sound "witchy" enough. As long as your intent is there, and you can visualize the results in your mind, you'll be fine.

CASTING A TEA SPELL

In this chapter, we will be casting tea spells, which are spells performed in front of a cup of tea or herbal brew to infuse your intentions into the liquid. This is meant to direct your intentions and give your spells and brews an extra "oomph" of power so you can manifest your results faster or with more impact. Tea spells are great because many spells require using certain herbs while casting. By consuming those herbs in a drink, you're taking in that magic, thus saving yourself a step. It also helps your own power of belief. You may be skeptical that saying a few words into the void will actually manifest something, but if you cast a spell into your brew and drink it, you are more likely to believe in that power because you are performing an action: you are drinking it.

One of the best things about spell casting is its versatility. There are many ways to cast a spell, from dramatic rituals to the mundane, with plenty of flexibility to do what works for your life. While the spells found in this chapter do have certain rituals, you can decide how far you want to go with them, from loud chanting and waving a magic wand to silently sipping your drink and saying a few words in your mind. As long as you have a clear intention about what you want to achieve, both will work.

We will also be incorporating modern technology or modern witch "hacks" into many of these spells. But if you're an old-school witch, feel free to do your craft as you see fit. Same for those who work with deities, are Wiccan, or practice paganism. However, if you are not into the religious or spiritual aspect of witchcraft, don't force yourself to add that into your spells. Your spells will work because you are putting your energy into them—that's what's important here.

THE FOUR COMPONENTS OF A SPELL

To make a spell work, there are four things you need to do: assert your will, state your intention, focus your energy, and take action.

1. **Assert Your Will.** Asserting your will is letting the universe know what you desire and what you are driven toward manifesting in your life. This isn't forcing the universe to give you what you want. Rather, your will in your own magical agenda is what you're driven to do with the powers you already have. For example, if you want career success, your will is to be successful, so you cast a prosperity spell. Whether the universe has that in store for you is another matter entirely. Still, you need to exert your willpower for a spell to work. Your spell should be your way of saying, "This is what I'm driven toward, and I'm going to make it happen with this spell." If you're wishy-washy about a spell ("I guess I want this," or "I don't think this will work but here goes nothing"), then you aren't going to get anything because you don't sound like you want it badly enough or believe in yourself enough to make it happen. Believe in your will. Believe in your magic.

2. **State Your Intention.** Despite all the imagery, metaphors, and powerful language, at its core, a spell is basically a contract between you and the universe. You are stating what you would like to manifest into reality and asking for it to happen. This is why it's

important to be clear about your intentions in your spell crafting and choose words that reflect that. For example, let's say you are looking for love, so you cast an attraction spell, hoping to meet a potential partner. However, you did not specify what type of people you want to be interested in you, and how many. Nor did you visualize your exact results. Suddenly you have tons of people blowing up your phone and DMs with texts from jerks who are obsessed with you. State your intentions with precise language: "I want $200 to pay my rent, and I want it by Thursday," or "I want someone nice and respectful to ask me on a date this month." That type of thing.

3. Focus Your Energy. This is a critical aspect of spell casting as you need to focus your energy on your intentions, or it won't happen. When you're distracted, your energies become scattered. You have to perform spells with feeling and focus, or they aren't going to work. This is why visualization and grounding before, during, and after casting is important. You need to be connected to your inner power.

4. Take Action. A spell needs action to be activated, whether it's by waving a wand, taking a drink, singing, dancing, or lighting a candle. This is because you need to expel energy to give your spell life. You also need to prove that you are willing to do some work to get what you desire. You are charging up your spell with your unique energy. By performing an action—doing a ritual, lighting a candle, making a drink—you are fulfilling your end of the contract. You're saying, in effect, "Look, I'm doing this; will you give me what I want?" And, as I mentioned before, it's easier to believe that you are actually manifesting something by physically doing something. By performing an action, you increase your own belief in yourself and in your magic.

> **MAGIC TRICK:** To make sure a spell never completely backfires in your face, include the phrase "for my highest good" at the end of any spell. That way, if a spell does backfire, you can avoid the drama and get something similar to what you want that is meant for you and good for your well-being. For example, say you cast a spell hoping for a promotion, but you don't get the promotion. You later talk to the person who got the promotion and discover has it has given them extra stress and longer hours with no extra pay. You later get an offer to work at a different company for more money and a better work-life balance. You saved yourself from getting a promotion that you would have hated and instead got a better opportunity, which is what you really needed. So always put a loophole in for yourself.

PLANNING YOUR SPELLS

Timing holds considerable importance in everything we do in life, and magic is no exception. Certain days of the week and phases of the moon hold unique magical properties that make them ideal for particular spells—and disastrous for other types. While you don't *need* to plan your spells around a certain day or phase of the moon (especially when you have to cast an emergency spell), using the magical correspondence of the day gives your spell a magical boost.

CASTING WITH THE LUNAR CYCLE

If you are interested in bringing the mystical magic of the moon into your craft, try planning your spells around the lunar calendar. Here is a quick overview of each moon phase in terms of spellwork.

NEW MOON: Cleansing spells, setting intentions, and performing divination.

WAXING CRESCENT: Manifesting, attraction, prosperity, and luck spells.

FIRST QUARTER: Strength, building momentum, fertility spells, and transformation spells.

WAXING GIBBOUS: Growth and protection spells, manifesting hopes and dreams.

FULL MOON: Charging, healing spells, and practicing gratitude.

WANING GIBBOUS: Cleansing and banishment.

THIRD QUARTER: Unbinding spells, introspection, sharing with others.

WANING CRESCENT: Scrying, meditation, self-care, and rest.

SEVEN DAYS OF MAGIC

If the lunar phases aren't your style, you can just use the calendar to plan out your spell. Each day of the week is associated with a planet, which has an influence on that day because each planet has its own magical correspondence that goes along with that day. Here is an overview:

MONDAY: Associated with the moon; good for fertility spells, divination, increasing dreams, and spirituality.

TUESDAY: Associated with Mars; good for spells associated with conquering obstacles, dealing with conflict, taking action, increasing energy, and gaining independence.

WEDNESDAY: Associated with Mercury; suitable for creativity spells, communication spells, job spells, and career spells.

THURSDAY: Associated with Jupiter; good for money spells, business spells, and legal matters.

FRIDAY: Associated with Venus; good for love spells, relationship spells, and sex spells.

SATURDAY: Associated with Saturn; good for protection spells, overcoming habits, banishing spells, binding spells, and meditation.

SUNDAY: Associated with the sun; good for success spells, abundance spells, strength, happiness spells, and healing spells.

SIGIL MAGIC

We have spent a great deal of this book looking into our teacups and trying to see symbols, but did you know that you can draw magical symbols on your teacups? That's right, if you aren't great at expressing yourself through writing, you can flex your artistic skills by using sigil magic.

Sigil magic is a type of spell that uses a symbol that someone has created that is charged with the intention of bringing about a specific outcome or magical property. While a spell uses words to achieve a result, with a sigil you infuse your magic into a drawing to create magic. The possibilities with sigils are endless; you can create one to attract a lover, to do well in school, for protection—the sky is the limit.

A sigil can look like anything and can be as complex or as simple as you want. Some people like to use runes as sigils, some like to create theirs based on their emotions, and some base them off their intent. You could also find sigils in your teacup by looking at the leaves and seeing what designs jump out at you for your intended purpose. Throughout these spells, I'll give you some sigil examples, but feel free to design your own.

> **MAGIC TRICK:** You can use sigil magic and herbal magic together by placing your sigil on the bottom of your teacup during spells, readings, or tea drinking. You can paint a protection or divination sigil on the outside of your teacup for a boost of intuition and security. If you're really good at latte art, create a sigil design in the foam and drink it. The possibilities are endless.

Now that you have a basic understanding of spell casting, let's get to the magic!

COME TO ME: A SIMPLE ATTRACTION SPELL

This is an easy-to-use spell that's perfect for beginners or people who just want a quick spell to use during the day, especially if they are interested in manifesting what they desire.

---

a mug

tea

a spoon

HOW TO CONJURE

STEP 1: Brew your tea.

STEP 2: As you wait for the tea to steep, think of three qualities you wish to attract. This should be very general, not "I want 300 dollars" or "I want a hot person to ask me out." Think about more general qualities, such as:

- ✶ Productivity, creativity, success
- ✶ Abundance, protection, peace
- ✶ Love, laughter, positivity
- ✶ Calmness, relaxation, happiness

Stick to only three.

STEP 3: Take your spoon and stir once, clockwise, while saying the first quality aloud. For example, if you are trying to attract creativity, you would say, "Creativity, come to me."

STEP 4: Repeat for the second and third quality.

STEP 5: When you stir for the final time, say, "As I drink this cup of tea, what I attract will be attracted to me."

STEP 6: Drink and enjoy.

FOR A DASH OF MAGIC

- Write a sigil of what you wish to attract, either on a piece of paper or directly into the brew using honey.

- If it goes with your tea, use a stick of cinnamon to stir as cinnamon brings good luck.

- Put a crystal that is associated with what you are trying to attract next to your cup. For example, if you are trying to attract love, use rose quartz. If you are trying to attract protection, use black tourmaline.

- Use "The Midas Blend" tea on page 55 for extra manifesting power.

- For best results, perform this spell during the waxing crescent moon or on a Sunday.

EVERYTHING WILL BE ALRIGHT:
A SPELL FOR CALMING AND REASSURANCE

Sometimes all we need to hear is that everything is going to be alright, even though we don't know exactly how. If you feel anxious, stressed, or unable to stop worrying, this spell will help you become grounded. Think of this as a warm hug in a mug assuring you that everything will be alright.

---

mug

tea *(see the "Tea Suggestions" on page 140 for recommendations)*

spoon

rose quartz

honey

HOW TO CONJURE

STEP 1: Prepare your tea as usual. If honey is usually added, save until the next step.

STEP 2: Add about half the honey you'd normally put in your tea and stir counterclockwise, saying, "I exile negative feelings, intrusive thoughts, and chaos from my mind, body, and heart." Exhale.

STEP 3: Add the rest of your honey and stir clockwise, saying, "I welcome peaceful thoughts, calming energy, and clarity into my mind, body, and heart." Inhale.

STEP 4: Pick up the rose quartz with your left hand; this is your receiving hand. Pick up the mug with your right hand; this is your giving hand.

STEP 5: As you watch the steam rise from your mug, imagine a white healing light coming from it. Imagine that light washing off your body, filling it with warmth and peace, pushing out the nervous energy. Exhale.

STEP 6: Now place the rose quartz in your right hand and the mug in your left hand.

STEP 7: Before taking your first sip, say, "Everything will be alright" three times.

STEP 8: Drink slowly and enjoy.

STEP 9: As you take your last sip, say, "For my highest good" to seal the energy.

FOR A DASH OF MAGIC

- If you are drinking this tea right before bed, take the rose quartz and put it under your pillow or next to your bed to promote sleep and good dreams.

- Perform this spell right after doing the "Should I Be Worried?" tea reading on page 116 if the reading caused you more anxiety than comfort.

- Put a protection sigil on the bottom of your cup, or write it into your tea with honey.

- For best results, perform this spell during a waning crescent moon.

TEA SUGGESTIONS

CHAMOMILE TEA: This is a great tea to have before bed, especially if your nervous thoughts are preventing you from sleeping or relaxing.

LEMON BALM TEA: This tea is famous for its ability to calm anxieties and reduce headaches, especially if they are stress-induced.

ANTI ANXIE-TEA: As it says in the name, this tea (see page 51) is made for reducing anxiety. Brew this to calm your nerves so you can truly believe that everything will be okay.

GOOD VIBES ONLY SPELL

We could all use a little positivity in our lives, especially when we hit some gloomy days. When positivity and good energy are hard to make on your own, call upon the spiritual vibration of the universe to bring you some good feelings. Because you just don't have time for bad vibes.

---❖---

tea

a cup

a good playlist

citrus-scented perfume, roll-on essential oil, citrus candle, or citrus incense *(positivity, good energy)*

1 stick of cinnamon *(happiness, good fortune)*

a sunny area or light-therapy lamp

---❖---

HOW TO CONJURE

STEP 1: Create your good vibe playlist. These should be songs that always manage to make you smile. It can be anything you want; don't be a music snob now. This playlist can be anything from cheesy pop tunes of the '00s to your favorite musical that no one has ever heard of. Hey, if screamo music makes you grin from ear to ear, put it on!

STEP 2: Once you have your playlist together, start playing it as you brew and prepare your tea. Feel free to dance around to the music as you do.

STEP 3: As your tea steeps, put on your citrus-scented perfume or roll-on essential oil, or light your citrus candle or incense stick. If you cannot stand the smell of citrus, put on your favorite perfume or burn your favorite candle.

STEP 4: When your tea has steeped, sit down in a sunny area. If it isn't sunny out or you can't get near the sunshine, sit in front of a light therapy lamp or wrap yourself up in a warm blanket in front of or under a light.

STEP 5: Take your cinnamon stick and stir your drink three times, clockwise. As you stir, say the following phrase three times: "I am moving to the rhythm of my highest vibration; all the energy that comes toward me today is positive. I only allow good vibes to enter my life."

STEP 6: Sip your drink while listening to your playlist. Jam out to the music: sing, dance, snap your fingers. Whatever puts you in a good mood.

STEP 7: When you have one sip left in your cup, say, "Good vibes from here on out," and drink, sealing the deal.

FOR A DASH OF MAGIC

- To increase your chances of having a good day, perform this spell while doing "The Daily Forecast" ritual on page 96.

- You can drink any type of tea for this spell, but if you want an extra boost of happiness, use the "Good-Thyme Tea" on page 53 or the "Negative Thought Repellent" on page 62.

- Perform this spell while wearing sunstone and smoky quartz or keeping those stones near you. Sunstone promotes positive thinking, while smoky quartz transforms negative energy into positive energy.

 Perform this spell outside, early in the morning if possible, to soak in some of the sun's good vibrations.

SWEETEN YOUR WORDS: A SPELL FOR DIFFICULT CONVERSATIONS

We all need to have difficult conversations in our lives, whether we're asking for a favor, apologizing for causing hurt feelings, or ending a relationship. As much as we'd like to wave a magic wand and skip all those hard conversations, they need to happen if we want to move forward in life. While we can't avoid difficult conversations, we can make them easier and even sway them in our favor. Here's a spell to help sweeten your words to get exactly what you want.

※
---

2 mugs (one for you and one for the other person)

enough tea for two people

vanilla-scented perfume or roll-on essential oil (opening your throat chakra, empowerment, mental strength, good luck)

2 teaspoons of honey (for smoothing things over and sweetness)

2 teaspoons of sugar (for smoothing things over)

※

HOW TO CONJURE

STEP 1: Call the person you need to have the conversation with and invite them to have tea with you. If you cannot have this conversation in person, either plan a phone or video call or have your phone nearby if you are having the conversation via text.

STEP 2: As you get ready for the meeting, make your tea and set a place for two people (even if you are doing this conversation over the phone).

STEP 3: Put on your vanilla perfume or roll-on essential oil, applying it to your neck at your throat and pulse points. If you are having a conversation via text, put the perfume on the pulse points of your wrists.

STEP 4: Just before your meeting, put a teaspoon of honey into your cup of tea, stirring it clockwise three times while saying these words with each stir: "With each sip, my words will flow like honey, allowing me to say my piece with peace. This conversation will move with ease."

STEP 5: Add a teaspoon of honey to the other person's drink, stirring it clockwise three times while saying these words with each stir: "I am open to hearing, I am open to change, I am open to listening to a new point of view."

STEP 6: Add a teaspoon of sugar to your cup, stirring it clockwise three times while saying these words with each stir: "My words come out with kindness and good intentions. My words bring the best outcome for everyone at my table."

STEP 7: Add a teaspoon of sugar to the other cup, stirring it clockwise three times while saying these words with each stir: "I come to this table in good faith and with good intentions. My armor is down, and I am without defenses. I am willing to listen and say my piece with added sweetness."

STEP 8: Just before the conversation, say aloud, "For the best of both parties," and tap your spoon on the rim of your cup.

STEP 9: Have the conversation. If the other person is not physically in the room, keep the cup in front of your laptop if you are doing a video call. If you're texting or having a phone call, place the cup in front of their picture or a personal item of theirs.

FOR A DASH OF MAGIC

✴ If you are worried about this conversation, use the "Negative Thought Repellent" blend on page 62. If you're looking to gain something from this conversation or really want this conversation to be successful, brew the "Confidence in a Cup" blend on page 70. If you feel you need a little extra protection during this conversation, brew the "Safe-tea First" tea on page 74 (and take other safety precautions in addition to magic).

✴ If you are performing this spell because you are having relationship issues or someone is being distant lately, perform "The Distance between Us" tea reading on page 113 to see what is wrong. It can help you prepare for this conversation.

✴ Add blue somewhere in your spell casting (blue cups, blue saucers, wearing blue, etc.). Not only is blue a calming color, which is ideal for a conversation that has the potential to get heated, but blue is also associated with the throat chakra. The throat chakra helps us communicate better, form ideas, and verbalize our feelings.

✴ If you're performing this spell because you're trying to get someone permanently out of your life, add a pinch of chamomile to their drink, not yours. Chamomile is for banishment—for getting someone out of your life for good without hard feelings.

MORE POWERFUL THAN YOU COULD EVER KNOW: A SPELL FOR CONFIDENCE AND TAKING ON THE WORLD LIKE A BADASS WITCH

When a witch, or anyone, connects with their personal magic and power, they are a force to be reckoned with. They can overcome every obstacle, fight a foe, or manifest their heart's desires.

However, most of us do not feel like this every day, or even regularly, despite our great power. On days when you don't feel like a confident, badass force of nature, and *really* need to feel like you are, cast this spell and step into your power.

---

tea *(enough for 2 cups)*

cup

2 index cards

pen

scissors

a citrine crystal *(stone of courage and confidence)*

a locket

HOW TO CONJURE

STEP 1: Prepare your drink, ideally the "Confidence in a Cup" blend on page 70, but anything that makes you feel prepared for the day will work.

STEP 2: As your drink steeps or cools down, place the citrine crystal in front of it.

STEP 3: When the cup is steeped and cool enough to drink, say these words as you stir three times, clockwise: "I am more powerful than anyone can possibly imagine. With each sip, I am becoming what I've always wanted to be."

STEP 4: Drink. As you drink, take one of your index cards and write down everything you wish to embody: intelligent, beautiful, forceful, direct, eloquent, courageous, even-tempered, talented, independent, etc. Be as imaginative as you want, but make sure you keep it short because you will need it to fit inside a locket. So, write small. Keep the citrine crystal on your paper.

STEP 5: When you get to the last sip, say aloud, "This is who I'm becoming, for my highest good." And drink.

STEP 6: Take your card and cut away the blank white area until just the list remains. Fold until it's tiny enough to fit into the locket.

STEP 7: Place your list into your locket and place it in a sunny area with your citrine crystal on top. For alternative options, see below.

STEP 8: Repeat steps one and two.

STEP 9: As you stir your new drink, say these words: "I've always been powerful. My magic has always lived in me. I honor and acknowledge the power in me."

STEP 10: Drink. As you drink, take the other index card and write down a list of everything you like about yourself. Things about yourself that you are proud of: kind, generous, intelligent, a good listener, a good sibling, witty, understanding, fearless, organized, etc. Really dig deep. If you can't think of anything, put "modest" down and see where you go from there.

STEP 11: When you get to your last sip of tea, say, "With this sip, I am reminding myself and others of my power. I am now connected to my untapped potential." And sip.

STEP 12: Put your new list in a safe place with the citrine.

STEP 13: Put on your locket and take on the world!

FOR A DASH OF MAGIC

- If your list is too big for your locket, draw a confidence sigil and put it in the locket instead. Put your list at your altar, in your notes app, or on a vision board.
- If you don't have a locket, type out your list on your notes app or email it to yourself.
- For an extra boost, perform this spell during the waxing crescent moon or on a Tuesday.
- Drink or eat something with ginger in it. Ginger is associated with confidence and power.

GETTING OUT OF HOT WATER:
A SPELL FOR GETTING OUT OF TROUBLE (OR AVOIDING IT IF YOU CAN)

Even the most magical of witches gets into uncomfortable situations now and again. And when we can't smooth things over with our words, we may try to get a little creative. Use this spell when you find yourself in trouble that you need to get out of.

————— ❖ —————

medium-sized cooking pot

spoon

ladle

teacup or mug

2 cups of water

1 teaspoon dried lemongrass *(cleansing and protection)*

1 teaspoon dried thyme *(smoothing things over)*

1 teaspoon dried passionflower *(calming and piece)*

————— ❖ —————

HOW TO CONJURE

STEP 1: Gather your supplies. Put your pot on the stove and pour in the water. Turn on the stove.

STEP 2: As you wait for the water to boil, visualize in your mind all the events that happened to lead you to the situation that you're in. Were there any mistakes made on your part? Were there mistakes made on someone else's part? See them bubble up to the surface and acknowledge it.

HERBAL TEA MAGIC *for the* **MODERN WITCH**

STEP 3: When the water has reached a boil, take the teaspoon of lemongrass and say, "With this lemongrass, I cleanse away the past. My future is protected," and put the herb in the pot.

STEP 4: Take the teaspoon of thyme and say, "With this thyme, I am ready to release the tension and turn over a new leaf," and put the herb in the pot.

STEP 5: Take the teaspoon of passionflower and say, "With this passionflower, I am calming the water, getting out the trouble that I'm in, and finding peace from the heat," and put the herb in the pot.

STEP 6: Take the water off the heat and turn off the stove. Take your ladle and put some of the brew in your cup.

STEP 7: Take your spoon and stir your drink three times, counterclockwise, saying the words, "With this brew, I'm banishing the bad, and finding my way to the other side," three times.

STEP 8: Drink. As you sip, meditate and ground yourself. How can you get out of the situation that you're in? What action do you need to take?

STEP 9: When you are at your last swallow of tea, say, "For my highest good," and drink to seal the spell.

FOR A DASH OF MAGIC

 If you are in legal trouble, add a teaspoon of calendula to your brew. Calendula represents protection in legal matters.

 Since this is loose leaf, you can also perform the "Should I Be Worried?" tea reading on page 116 to see just how much trouble you are currently in. Or you can perform the "Reveal Yourself!" reading on page 124.

 You can also turn this into a bath spell by making yourself a hot bath and putting the herbs in. When you're ready to get out of the tub, say these words: "I am getting out of hot water and moving on with my life with peace, protection, and a clean slate."

LET ME F*CKING SLEEP: A SPELL FOR TURNING OFF YOUR MIND AND CATCHING SOME STRESS-FREE SLEEP

There are some days (perhaps more often than not) where you just can't get to sleep. You toss and turn, but you just can't seem to hit the "off" button on your mind. Maybe you are nervous about something, have nightmares, or feel so burnt out that you're too tired to sleep. Whatever the case may be, this spell will hopefully put you into dreamland.

---

a mug of tea (*preferably the "Sweet Dreams Draught" on page 72*)

a sachet bag

a sprig of lavender (*for calming and to aid in sleep*)

3 leaves of lemon verbena (*protection from nightmares*)

1 tablespoon dried chamomile (*for calming and peace*)

a moonstone (*for sleep*)

HOW TO CONJURE

STEP 1: Brew your cup of tea that is warm and soothing.

STEP 2: As you wait for your drink, take your sachet bag, and put the lavender, lemon verbena, chamomile, and moonstone into it.

STEP 3: Tie the bag closed, hold it close to your chest, and repeat these words three times: "Tonight, as I lay my head to sleep, I'll shut my eyes and find sound sleep. And when I open them once again, my eyes will be rising with the sun."

STEP 4: Place the sachet under your pillow.

STEP 5: Get your drink and climb into bed. Drink your tea in bed, putting your phone away, and keeping your lights low. As you sip, imagine the soft, soothing energy flowing through you. Imagine yourself slowly powering off and ready for sleep.

STEP 6: When you get to your last sip of tea, say, "And now, just let me go the f*ck to sleep, I'm a very tired witch."

STEP 7: Witch, go the f*ck to sleep!

FOR A DASH OF MAGIC

🌙 If you're having trouble falling asleep due to nightmares, add mugwort to your sachet.

🌙 If you're having trouble falling asleep because you are dealing with negative thoughts, brew the "Negative Thought Repellent" on page 62 before bed.

🌙 If music helps you fall asleep, put on a calming sleep playlist while you drink your brew. Hum the music as you sip to infuse the comforting magic into your brew.

KARMA WITCHES: A HEX THAT GIVES PEOPLE EXACTLY WHAT'S COMING TO THEM

When it comes to witchcraft, the general rule of thumb is that hexes and jinxes are frowned upon for various reasons. Some (mainly Wiccans) believe that by hexing someone, you are invoking the threefold rule, where if you cast a spell to hurt someone, you get that negative aspect returned to you threefold. Some believe that it's wrong to use witchcraft against others because you are using your powers against someone who doesn't use their magic, creating an unfair advantage. I believe it's unfair to curse or hex someone simply because you don't like them, or they got something you wanted, or they turned you down. However, if someone has been purposely cruel or unkind, has wielded their privilege to hurt others, or has done harm without empathy, it may be time to pull some magic. This spell is meant to bring about karma to someone who has done *true harm* without facing the consequences as of yet. You do not get to decide the punishment, but merely to push karma along a little quicker.

---·❄·---

pen and paper
a cup of tea
a purple candle (*the color associated with justice*)
a fireproof container
the Justice tarot card (*from a deck you're not using or printed out from the internet*)

---·❄·---

HOW TO CONJURE

STEP 1: Take your pen and paper and write down all the bad things the person you have in mind has done. Make a list of everything this person has done to you and others. Put the person's name at the top of the list.

STEP 2: Brew your drink.

STEP 3: Light the candle.

STEP 4: Take your piece of paper in your hands and say, "(Insert person's name here), you did the sowing, and now it's time for the reaping. I don't wish bad things—only what is owed."

STEP 5: Burn, baby, burn (light at least a corner of the paper with the candle).

STEP 6: Place the note in the fireproof container to burn itself out.

STEP 7: Drink your brew. As you sip, imagine justice—not what kind of punishment you want for this person or what you want karma to look like for them, but what justice would look like to you. An apology? Money? A public acknowledgment of wrongdoing? Never seeing them again because they respect your boundaries? What is justice to you?

STEP 8: When the note has been burned, put out the fire by pouring the rest of your drink into the container (if your drink is still hot, use water). As you put the fire out, say these words: "I pour out the fire of my hurt; may justice be finally served."

STEP 9: When the ashes have cooled, place them in a different container behind or beneath the Justice card. When karma has finally come to this person, you can dump the ashes.

FOR A DASH OF MAGIC

🌙 Use tea with ginger in it or a ginger herbal brew for this spell as ginger is associated with retribution.

🌙 Do a tea reading to find out what when karma will finally come and what it may look like.

🌙 If you don't do fires or candles, you can use a flameless candle for the ritual and tear the paper into tiny pieces and save them instead of burning them.

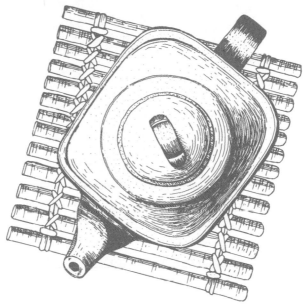

LET GO AND LET GROW: A MOVING-ON SPELL

Doing a complete 180 from "Karma Witches," if you want to move on from the past and embrace the future, try this spell. Whether you're letting go of a past relationship, a career that didn't work, or pain from the past that has been difficult to heal from, this spell will help you discover that to move on, you'll need some thyme.

---

leaves from outside

pen/marker

plant labels

thyme seeds

a pot and some soil

HOW TO CONJURE

STEP 1: Gather some leaves from outdoors that you can write on with a pen or marker. This will be easy in the fall, but if you are doing this spell in other seasons, use what's available: for instance, you may pick green leaves from plants in the spring, and in the winter you may write in the snow with your fingers. Or simply do the next step on your phone.

STEP 2: Choose about five things that you want to let go of in your life, and write one down on each leaf. These can be anything: moving on from a relationship, letting go of other people's expectations, letting go of perfection, leaving a job, etc.

STEP 3: Go outside with your leaves. Stand facing south and say, "I'm letting go of all that is no longer serving me. I'm releasing this burden and moving on."

STEP 4: Let go of the leaves and watch them drift away (if you wrote them in the snow, erase it; if you typed them on your phone, delete it).

STEP 5: Take your thyme seeds, your soil, and your pot and get planting. If you have a backyard, plant it there. If you have a tiny space, plant the thyme in a windowsill herb garden or in its own pot by the window.

STEP 6: When you plant your seeds, take up to five plant labels and write what you want to grow: self-love, a new career, confidence, family, etc. You can even write them as sigils. When you finish, put them into your pot.

STEP 7: Before watering your plant, say, "With this water, I'm growing the life that I want. I'm giving this time and attention to move forward in my life." Then water.

STEP 8: Continue to take care of your plant as it grows, allowing your new life to flourish.

FOR A DASH OF MAGIC

- When the thyme gets large enough to harvest, use it in teas, spells, or kitchen magic.
- Depending on your intentions, you can swap thyme for other herbs and flowers (see Chapter Two for more information on the magical properties of various herbs).

🌍 When you're planting your thyme, drink "The Midas Blend" on page 55 to get what you want faster.

🌍 If you are nervous about letting go, do the "Where Am I Going?" tea reading (page 119) or the "Seasons Change and So Do I" ritual (page 106) for guidance.

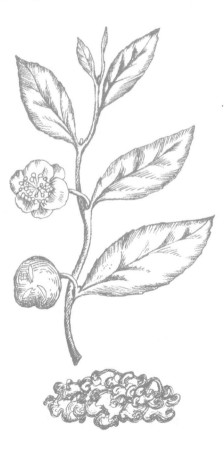

HERBAL TEA MAGIC *for the* **MODERN WITCH**

LOVE ME, LOVE ME: A SPELL FOR BRINGING LOVE INTO YOUR LIFE

As I have mentioned many times throughout this book, love spells are unethical because they go against a person's consent. However, if you are trying to attract love into your life, this spell can help. We've covered potions and readings, but as you'll see, this quick spell uses herbs in a different way.

---

1 handful of fresh rose petals

1 tablespoon of coconut oil

mortar and pestle

water

HOW TO CONJURE

STEP 1: Using your mortar and pestle, crush your rose petals into a fine paste.

STEP 2: Add in your coconut oil and mix until a fine paste is formed.

STEP 3: Get ready to take a shower or bath. You can also do the following steps near your bathroom or a bowl of water.

STEP 4: Dab the paste with the tips of your fingers and write words on your skin: your arms, legs, stomach, wherever! Write what you bring to the relationship: humor, passion, stability, a home, etc. Draw a sigil if you prefer.

STEP 5: Wash off the words with the water, imagining your words and desires going into the universe.

STEP 6: Dry off and go on with your day.

FOR A DASH OF MAGIC

🫖 After doing this spell, drink the "Love Potion No. 9" on page 59 to attract romance faster.

🫖 Perform the "Who Is My Next Lover?" tea reading on page 109 to see who is coming into your life.

🫖 Perform this spell on a Friday as it is ruled by Venus.

🫖 You can also use hibiscus flowers instead of rose petals as hibiscus is associated with love and lust.

🫖 Make this paste before a date and dab a little on your skin for extra magic.

★ ★ ★

And remember, spells are flexible, so don't feel you have to use the same wording or the exact same rituals as what's written here. Do what feels comfortable for you.

Chapter 7

WRITTEN IN THE STARS: TASSEOGRAPHY AND ASTROLOGY

*H*ey, baby, what's your sign? Astrology is the study of the astronomical positions of the planets, asteroids, and stars and their correlation with events on Earth, often used for divination purposes. While many of us know our sun sign and read horoscopes, astrology is much more complex. It needs close study of the planetary movements to understand how events may unfold and even how to understand ourselves.

So, how does tasseography come into play? I mean, you can't see the cosmos in your teacup (if you do, you may need glasses). While that's true, you can do a lot with astrology in herbal magic, from creating special tea to using the zodiac wheel to predict the future at the bottom of your cup. Here are a few methods of infusing astrology into herbalism and tasseography practices.

ASTROLO-TEA

Just as herbs have their own magical qualities, the zodiac signs are each associated with certain herbs. The zodiac signs also have corresponding body parts that can cause the sign a lot of problems, from Taurus's famous sore throats to Virgo's tummy trouble. Here are some tea blends that best correspond with the signs—both in personality and in need.

Each of these tea blends makes twenty-four cups of tea for you to enjoy.

> **MAGIC TRICK:** Along with your sun sign, also check your moon and rising sign for your tea blend; you may like one better than the other.

ARIES (MARCH 20–APRIL 19)

Courageous, confident, and possessing a lust for life that cannot be beat, Aries needs a tea that matches their fiery nature, fueling their inner passion while soothing their equally famous temper. Look for herbs that bring headache relief as Aries rules the head.

¾ cup gunpowder green tea (*green tea represents Aries's fire element and helps heal headaches; gunpowder green tea has a smoky taste and gives an extra boost of alertness*)

1 teaspoon ground cinnamon (*associated with Aries and fire; lowers blood pressure*)

> **1 teaspoon whole cloves** (*provides Aries with some much-needed protection and banishes bad energy*)
>
> **½ teaspoon red peppercorn** (*represents Aries's signature color and relieves energy blocks*)
>
> ———— ❖ ————

TAURUS (APRIL 20–MAY 20)

Dependable, steady, and ever resourceful, Taurus may have a reputation for a strong stubborn streak, but they are sensual and affectionate when you get past their walls. Ruled by lovely Venus, Taurus needs a tea blend that feels luxurious but isn't too pricey. And anything that helps with a sore throat is always a requirement.

> ———— ❖ ————
>
> **½ cup vanilla black tea** (*black tea is associated with the earth element, while vanilla is associated with Venus*)
>
> **½ cup dried rose petals** (*associated with Venus; promotes healing, glamour, love, and luck*)
>
> **½ teaspoon ground cardamom** (*associated with Taurus; good for providing direction, wisdom, and clarity*)
>
> **½ tablespoon fresh or dried thyme** (*helps with sore throats and coughs*)
>
> ———— ❖ ————

GEMINI (MAY 21–JUNE 20)

Curious, witty, and famous for their gift of gab, Geminis are versatile and adaptable, which is great for multitasking but can make them a little flighty as they have so many ideas going on at once. Gemini needs a blend that can keep their energy up but also help them focus so they can actually get things done.

⅓ cup **white tea** (*associated with the air element; promotes clarity, realization, and wisdom*)

¼ cup **dried lavender** (*associated with the planet Mercury; helps ease anxiety and promotes relaxation*)

¼ cup **peppermint** (*helps reduce upper respiratory infections, as Gemini rules the lungs; boosts metal clarity and positive thoughts*)

¼ cup **lemongrass** (*relieves anxiety; promotes emotional growth and clarity*)

CANCER (JUNE 21–JULY 22)

Imaginative, nurturing, and sentimental, Cancer needs an herbal blend that is as sweet as they are while providing some mood boosting for their crabbier side. Protective and empathic, Cancers have psychic abilities that could always use a boost.

¼ cup **oolong tea** (*associated with the water element, it improves gut health and helps with emotional balance, serenity, and divination*)

¼ cup **lemon verbena** (*promotes love, strength, and protection from nightmares*)

¼ cup **dried cornflower** (*relieves chest congestion; promotes protection, spirituality, growth, and creativity; also makes your tea blue, which is Cancer's color*)

¼ cup **strawberry leaf** (*improves heart health; promotes love, happiness, and friendship*)

LEO (JULY 23–AUGUST 22)

The royalty of the jungle, a Leo always makes their presence known with a bold presence, dramatic style, and entertaining vibes. They need a tea blend that as vibrant as they are but can also get them up and moving when they feel like lazing in the sun. With a generous heart, they always make enough to share for their whole pride.

⅓ cup green tea *(associated with the fire element, it improves heart health—Leo rules the heart—and is associated with passion, energy, and mindfulness)*

⅓ cup dried calendula *(associated with the sun, Leo's ruling planet; also great for taking care of your luscious mane)*

¼ tablespoon dried orange peel *(associated with Leo; also brings both love and luck)*

½ tablespoon dried ginger *(boosts confidence; increases energy, personal power, and passion)*

VIRGO (AUGUST 23–SEPTEMBER 22)

Analytical, sensible, and always willing to lend a helping hand, Virgos have a lot of nervous energy (as they always need to have a plan), so they need a tea that can relax them and give them peace of mind. Teas and herbs that help calm an upset stomach should always be within arm's reach because you'll never catch a Virgo unprepared.

½ cup decaffeinated black tea (*associated with the earth element, it relieves stress while decreasing digestive activity; decaffeinated so Virgo can finally get some rest*)

¼ cup dried spearmint (*eases nausea; brings positive thoughts, healing, protection, and relaxation*)

¼ cup blackberry leaf (*brings healing, money, and protection*)

1 tablespoon dried licorice root (*increases feelings of empowerment*)

LIBRA (SEPTEMBER 23–OCTOBER 22)

Romantic, charming, and ever elegant, Libra needs a delicate tea that enchants their Venus-ruled taste buds, but that also looks good. It always should have a variety of things so Libra never has to make up their mind. Sociable and fair, Libra always makes sure there's enough for everyone.

⅓ cup white tea (*associated with the air element, it helps with skin damage, mediation, happiness, and protection*)

⅓ cup red rooibos leaves (*helps create glowing skin, brings out strength and inner peace and grounding; also creates a lovely rosy color that Libras love*)

¼ cup dried passionflower (*boosts friendship, love, and peace*)

1 tablespoon mugwort (*supports liver health, divination, and spiritual cleansing*)

SCORPIO (OCTOBER 23–NOVEMBER 22)

Passionate and driven, with a touch of mystery, Scorpio is a force to be reckoned with. While they can easily become obsessed with any blend that catches their fancy, they need something as strong and seductive as they are. They need a mysterious and tempting brew to drive them as they plot their next scheme.

----------·❉·----------

⅓ cup oolong tea *(associated with the water element and autumn; improves moods, creates emotional balance, and helps with divination)*

⅓ cup dried hibiscus flower *(helps reduce depression; helps with menstrual cramps—as Scorpio rules the reproductive system; promotes lust, peace, divination, and passion)*

⅓ cup raspberry leaf *(relieves cramps; boosts confidence, healing, and joy)*

2 teaspoons ground ginseng *(boosts mood; increases sex drive; associated with lust, vitality, protection, and wishes)*

----------·❉·----------

SAGITTARIUS (NOVEMBER 23–DECEMBER 21)

Optimistic, honest, and always up for an adventure, Sagittarius needs the right blend to fuel their many spontaneous travel plans and philosophical discussions—while also moderating their more impulsive tendencies. This blend will help Sagittarius keep up their energy without burning themselves out.

½ cup jasmine green tea (*green tea is associated with the fire element and promotes mindfulness, regulating energy, and clarity; jasmine is associated with Sagittarius*)

⅓ cup dandelion root (*brings wish-granting, good luck, and divination*)

1 teaspoon ground nutmeg (*brings travel, luck, and psychic ability*)

2 pieces star anise (*brings happiness, luck, and protection*)

CAPRICORN (DECEMBER 22–JANUARY 19)

Ambitious, disciplined, and responsible, this ultimate earth sign is already prepared to get stuff done, so what Capricorn needs is a tea blend that's ready to get down to business. Something that will give them energy for their world-domination plans, but also helps them feel more optimistic that their plans will work.

¼ cup black tea (*associated with the earth element, it also improves bone health—Capricorn rules the skeletal system; promotes stability and grounding; expels negativity*)

¼ cup dried chamomile (*prevents osteoporosis; promotes prosperity, love, and peaceful vibes*)

¼ cup yerba mate (*boosts physical and mental energy; associated with insight, bonding, and friendship*)

¼ cup dried blueberries (*calming, passion, protection, and associated with earth*)

AQUARIUS (JANUARY 20-FEBRUARY 18)

Independent, friendly, and ever the eccentric, Aquarius is always ready to think outside the teacup with their innovative attitude. While they can be a little aloof and unpredictable at times, the right cup of tea can help warm them up (especially since they always need to warm up their circulatory system).

⅓ **cup white tea** (*associated with the air element; also associated with happiness, wisdom, blessings, and protection*)

⅓ **cup diced dried pineapple** (*associated with creativity, happiness, and memory*)

2 tablespoons fennel seeds (*fights colds; brings courage, love, and divination*)

1 tablespoon grated fresh turmeric (*improves memory, eases depression symptoms, and brings protection and health*)

PISCES (FEBRUARY 19-MARCH 20)

Imaginative, gentle, and unselfish to a fault, Pisces are a true inspiration for how we should all treat each other with kindness. However, Pisces need to remember to take care of themselves as their self-sacrificing nature and impracticality can leave them a little vulnerable. They need a tea blend that allows them to put up their feet and rest.

⅓ **cup oolong tea** *(associated with the water element; improves mood; brings emotional balance, connection, wisdom, friendships, and serenity)*

⅓ **cup dried elderflower** *(brings protection, prosperity, psychic awareness, grounding, joy, and emotional healing)*

⅓ **cup dried lemon balm** *(brings success, healing, and spiritual development)*

2 **tablespoons dried apple, diced** *(associated with love, divination, and spirituality)*

ZODIAC WHEEL READING

In astrology, the twelve zodiac signs are placed on a circle known as the zodiac or astrology wheel. The wheel acts similar to a clock, where the planets and asteroids are moving clockwise through each sign's section on the wheel. The zodiac wheel is how we plot out our birth charts, which help guide us in understanding future events. You can also use the zodiac wheel in your tea reading. In fact, there are many special fortune-telling cups that have the zodiac wheel on the saucer and the planetary symbols inside the cup. However, you can also do this on your own like a regular tea reading.

Here a few examples.

ASTROLOGICAL YEAR READING:
PREDICTING THE YEAR AHEAD

Similar to "The Year Ahead" ritual on page 103, you can also predict the year ahead by using the zodiac wheel, dividing your cup into twelve sections, but replace the months with zodiac signs. However, if you want a more in-depth reading, try this:

---※---

cup and saucer

tea *(preferably the tea blend that matches your sun sign)*

a copy of the current astrology calendar

pen and paper

---※---

THE READING

STEP 1: Take your saucer and, mentally or on a piece of paper, divide it into twelve sections, one section for each sign. Take your cup and divide it into seven sections to represent the planets (which in astrology includes the sun and the moon), like so:

STEP 2: Do your reading as you normally would, while leaving a little bit more tea in your cup in order to get some more on your saucer.

STEP 3: When studying your reading, pay close attention to both the saucer and the cup, taking note of where the tea lands and what it looks like. For example, if you have a lot going on in your Mercury section, you may have a lot of difficulty with Mercury's retrograde this year. If you have a boat shape in both Venus and Leo, you may be going on a trip when Venus is in Leo. This reading will require a lot of playing around, so give yourself plenty of room for trial and error with your predication. Use the astrology calendar as a guide.

FOR A DASH OF MAGIC

While the regular calendar begins the new year on January 1, the astrological new year doesn't begin until April 20 with the start of Aries season, so do this reading around that time.

PREDICTING SOMEONE'S BIRTH CHART

After trying to predict who your next lover will be, you can try predicting the birth chart of a future lover or soul mate, or even of your future children. This is not the easiest reading to do as you'll have to do a lot of mixing and matching to see what fits and makes sense. But if you're not basing your entire dating life on what you see in a teacup (and please, don't do that), this could be a fun game and a way to test your predicting and astrology skills.

---

cup and saucer

tea

pen and paper

an astrology chart or astrology app *(optional)*

THE READING

STEP 1: Do the same thing you did in the astrology year reading: divide your saucer into twelve sections, but instead of dividing the cup into seven sections for the planets, divide it into eight sections, using the handle to indicate where the rising sign will be.

STEP 2: Continue your regular tea reading ritual. If you would like, imagine your ideal partner or child. Picture them in your mind as you sip.

STEP 3: Do the rest of your ritual, making sure there are some tea leaves on the saucer and in the cup. See what signs have leaves on them and how much tea is spread out on the planets. For example, if you have a lot of tea leaves on Taurus, that birth chart may have a lot of planets in Taurus. If there are a lot of tea clumps on the sun, Mercury, and Mars sections, the birth chart may feature the sun, Mercury, and Mars being in Taurus. Also, if you see similar patterns, put them together. For example, if you see a circle in Venus and a circle in Sagittarius, your future partner may have their Venus in Sagittarius. Use your astrology app to try out some of the possible birth charts you've found and see what pairing may actually work. For example, it's impossible for someone to have a Virgo sun with an Aries Mercury because Mercury changes signs every two weeks (along with retrogrades), but you can have a Virgo sun and an Aries moon because the moon moves through a sign every two days. So, play a little to see what makes sense.

ZODIAC WHEEL: HOUSES

Along with the twelve astrology signs, the zodiac wheel also contains twelve houses where each sign rules. Each house represents different things like this:

HERBAL TEA MAGIC *for the* **MODERN WITCH**

While the other two rituals dealt with timing and possible traits of a person, the house wheel can help you answer certain types of questions, such as: What areas in life do I need to improve in? What areas will become a major focus soon? What areas should I pay more attention to? They are a way to help you look at different areas of your life and how you can best help yourself now—and in the future.

WITCH TIP: When dividing up your astrology houses in your cup, make sure your fourth house is where your cup handle is because the fourth house deals with home and family, and the handle represents home.

ONE FINAL DASH OF MAGIC

That's right, witches, we are finally at the end of our journey together. However, while this is the end of this book, I hope it is the beginning of your own personal journey of herbal magic, tasseography, kitchen witchcraft, or just learning to appreciate the magic in all things—from a cup of tea to affirming words that you whisper to yourself. I hope this book has taught you not just the meaning of peppermint and lavender, and how to predict your day at the bottom of your cup, but how to find magic everywhere, especially in the mundane, where you sprinkle cinnamon in your coffee and face the world.

But, more than anything, I hope this has helped you remember that you are magic.

SYMBOL DICTIONARY

From acorns to zebras, if you are curious about the symbols you see in your cup, you've come to the right place. While this guide provides the general meaning of each symbol and the meaning of its placement in your cup, keep in mind that your interpretation is just as important because tea readings are deeply personal. So, if you see a dog and you have a dog, the cups may be talking about your pet rather than a friendship. Remember, tasseography is a story the universe is trying to tell you—symbols just act as a guide to help tell the story.

ACORN

General meaning: Usually a favorable symbol, representing new beginnings or "planting a seed" for something new to grow. It's a symbol of freedom and having the power to bring things to life, from creative projects, to wealth, to spiritual renewal.

When it's at the top of the cup: A new beginning! A birth of something significant in your life: a child, relationship, business, or creative project. Major opportunity.

When it's on the sides of the cup: Success in business and good health.

When it's at the bottom of the cup: If you missed an opportunity recently, you may get another shot at it!

When it's near the handle: You may come into some money in the future, probably within two to three months. Money will improve your life. Think "seed money."

Broken acorn: If the acorn is broken, you may struggle with success in your new projects. You'll have to find a new way of doing things.

AIRPLANE

General meaning: While our first thought when seeing an airplane in our cup is travel (and it may be that if you are going on a trip), seeing an airplane symbolizes an unexpected visitor, or a project that may or may not work out in your favor.

When it's at the top of the cup: Career advancements are coming your way very soon.

When it's on the sides of the cup: Avoiding work you must do, projects going unfinished.

When it's at the bottom of the cup: Projects not going well, losing money or source of income, something is holding you back.

When it's near the handle: Some news is coming from someone who lives far away.

Crashed airplane: Withdraw from being in the public eye for the moment. Keep your life private for now.

Airplane surrounded by clouds: Take a passionate approach to life.

ALLIGATOR

General meaning: See you later, alligator. Seriously, when you spy an alligator, you'll want it to go away. Alligators symbolize danger and personal misfortune coming your way. It could also be a warning that someone close to you is the source of your problem and they aren't who they appear to be.

When it's at the top of the cup: Using other people to escape a difficult relationship.

When it's on the sides of the cup: Be on your guard. A friend could turn into a foe.

When it's at the bottom of the cup: Fighting against hidden enemies.

When it's near the handle: You'll need to respond quickly to a difficult situation in your career.

ANCHOR

General meaning: When upright, the anchor is usually a favorable symbol, representing good, loyal friends, steady romantic relationships, and having realistic goals come true. If you are at sea, this is usually a symbol of safety. However, if the anchor is upside down, it means instability and the feeling of sinking or drowning. Sink or swim.

When it's at the top of the cup: If you see an anchor at the top of the cup, this can represent good progress in your relationships, including business, friend, and romantic relationships. You are "rising to the top." However, this comes with a word of warning to not be dependent on others for your happiness.

When it's on the sides of the cup: You're going to have to make some important decisions when it comes to your work or business. A real "sink or swim" moment. Could also mean traveling by water.

When it's at the bottom of the cup: If the anchor is near the bottom of the cup but not in the center, it indicates some instability in your relationships, some rough waters ahead. If it's in the center of the bottom of the cup, it means you will find the solution to your problems if you ask your friends for help.

When it's near the handle: Good luck and a positive outcome.

Dots around the anchor: Roll up your sleeves and get to work.

ANGEL

General meaning: This is a very positive symbol, representing good news in matters of love and creativity. It can also represent spiritual protection, moral support, and financial backing.

When it's at the top of the cup: An increase of intuition, being productive, and finding peace in life.

When it's on the sides of the cup: Good news is coming!

When it's at the bottom of the cup: Sign that an illness is coming—either you are getting sick or someone else is.

When it's near the handle: You may get emotionally hurt by someone you care about.

APPLE

General meaning: An apple a day keeps the doctor away, but seeing an apple in your teacup could mean some pleasant things are heading your way. Apples symbolize learning, education, and being studious, so it could mean you are going back to school. On the other side, apple is known as the "forbidden fruit" and symbolizes temptation and passion. Either way, it's an educational experience.

When it's at the top of the cup: Here the apple represents new beginnings, such as a new relationship or a new chapter in your life. This will be happening very quickly, so get ready!

When it's on the sides of the cup: Succumbing to temptation in life, but the consequences won't be as bad as you think.

When it's at the bottom of the cup: Encouraging you to do things that will make you healthier and expand your intellectual horizons. Could manifest itself in different eating habits, working out, taking care of yourself, going back to school, or taking classes.

When it's near the handle: Emotional happiness and improving personal relationships.

Half-eaten apple: Compromise is needed.

Two apples together: Coming into money.

ARROW

General meaning: Ready, aim, fire! The arrow is the symbol of direction, movement, and progress. When shooting an arrow, one must take aim, pull the bowstring back, and let go as the arrow launches into the air. This can represent movement through life, knowing your target, and being determined to get there. However, it also represents the need for self-discipline. After all, if you aren't focused on where you're pointing your arrow, you could end up heading in the wrong direction—or hurting something. In astrology, Sagittarius is represented by the archer, so the arrow could represent the presence of a Sagittarius.

When it's at the top of the cup: Good news is coming your way! Usually about a love affair or making a good choice that has affected people positively.

When it's on the sides of the cup: Could be overwhelmed with emotions and confused about where to turn. Feeling a little directionless.

When it's at the bottom of the cup: You have the power to change your direction in your life. Your fate is in your hands. All you have to do is take aim and move. You have a lot of power if you're willing to use it.

When it's near the handle: Very emotional time. Becoming connected with loved ones and family members.

Direction of the arrow: The direction of the arrow is just as important as the placement. If the arrow is pointing up, you are going in the right direction and your aim is true. Pointing down means you've lost your focus or are stuck.

AXE

General meaning: When an axe appears in your teacup, it's time to do some cutting—whether you are cutting toxic people from your life or cutting major deals with people. It also represents overcoming problems, taking the lead, and handling whatever is coming your way. You got this.

When it's at the top of the cup: Needing to heal wounds that happened long ago. Trying to move on from feelings of anger and sadness.

When it's on the sides of the cup: The need to use a creative outlet to overcome an emotionally turbulent time.

When it's at the bottom of the cup: Family issues, attempting to break away from a difficult situation, needing to take control of your own life.

When it's near the handle: You have everything you need to overcome your current problems.

BABY

General meaning: Obviously, the first thing you may think of when you see a baby in your teacup is an actual baby. However, before you start buying baby clothes and picking out names (or totally freaking out), relax—a tea reading isn't a pregnancy test. While it could mean a literal baby, a baby in tasseography usually represents a new project, new beginnings, and happier times in your life. Basically, just some additional joy in your life.

When it's at the top of the cup: New opportunities will be coming to you very soon. Being in a joyful place in life after getting rid of negativity. Possible pregnancy (though this is not a pregnancy test).

When it's on the sides of the cup: Achievement in anything you put your mind to.

When it's at the bottom of the cup: A need for a rebirth of some kind. Spiritual and material needs are not being met. New opportunities lead to trouble.

When it's near the handle: The need to take on new responsibilities.

BIRD

General meaning: A bird is always a good symbol, representing good travel and protection from negative forces, and a sign that a change is coming into your life. Just as birds continually migrate throughout the year, you are taking flight and going on a new journey of your own.

When it's at the top of the cup: It's okay to take flight right now; you are being protected.

When it's on the sides of the cup: Good time to travel.

When it's at the bottom of the cup: There could be a dangerous situation coming your way. Not a great time to travel as you must stay on your toes.

When it's near the handle: New beginnings are on their way. A major, but positive, change is on the horizon.

Flying birds: Breaking away from a bad situation. Becoming free.

Bird in a cage: Feeling trapped.

Bird's nest: Happy times in your home and intimate relationships.

BOAT

General meaning: Seeing a boat in your teacup represents a voyage of some sort—you may be going on a trip, or a friend will be visiting you shortly.

When it's at the top of the cup: A good friend is coming to visit you for a few days. Can also refer to overseas travel.

When it's on the sides of the cup: Taking a trip would be beneficial to your overall health.

When it's at the bottom of the cup: Other people's emotions could get the better of you. Spend some time alone.

When it's near the handle: You're about to start a new hobby. You may have trouble with your hobby at first, but you will be very successful later.

BOTTLE

General meaning: While seeing a bottle in your cup can mean a variety of things (for example, seeing a baby bottle is very different from seeing a wine bottle). Usually, seeing a bottle represents a need to focus on one's health and getting well. It can also mean looking ahead to the future.

When it's at the top of the cup: Dealing with issues with clients or friendship problems.

When it's on the sides of the cup: Health is improving but may take a while.

When it's at the bottom of the cup: A new beginning will happen very quickly.

When it's near the handle: Good health in the long term.

Baby bottle: Dealing with someone who is very childish.

Wine bottle: Having a difficult time in your life.

BOUQUET

General meaning: Love is in the air (and in the cup) when you see a bouquet as it represents happier times ahead: positive relationships, success, and being lucky in love. It can also be a symbol of marriage.

When it's at the top of the cup: Happy days! A time for marriage proposals, falling in love, and feeling on top of the world.

When it's on the sides of the cup: You need to focus on your relationships right now.

When it's at the bottom of the cup: You need to do some work in order to recognize your full potential. On the road to recovery.

When it's near the handle: Hiding from love and romance. Possible commitment issues.

BRIDGE

General meaning: Bridges are made to connect two places, and when you see a bridge in your reading, it can symbolize building a bridge between you and another person, or it can represent traveling to a new location. Whether you are connecting new ideas or building new connections and understandings, the bridge is a positive symbol. It can also represent connecting the past to the present or connecting reality with fantasy.

When it's at the top of the cup: Encouraging you to use your imagination more. If you are doing a career reading, this can mean you would do well in a career that allows you to use your creative talents.

When it's on the sides of the cup: You will reach your destination.

When it's at the bottom of the cup: Your troubles will be over soon; some higher power will come in to save the day—just have faith.

When it's near the handle: Reconnecting with an old friend.

BUS

General meaning: All aboard! Next stop: the future! Seeing a bus is a positive symbol in tea readings as you are going on a journey in your life, moving from one phase to the next. While it can be an uncertain or tense time, with hard work you can make the transition as smooth as possible.

When it's at the top of the cup: Anxiously waiting for results or a decision to be made.

When it's on the sides of the cup: People are willing to help you with your goals.

When it's at the bottom of the cup: It may take a long time to reach your goals.

When it's near the handle: Positive news is coming.

BUTTERFLY

General meaning: The butterfly is a symbol of a transformation of sorts: physical, spiritual, and emotional. A time of growth and rebirth.

When it's at the top of the cup: The best placement for the butterfly, meaning that happiness is near. Could also represent a spiritual awakening or increased intuition.

When it's on the sides of the cup: Can symbolize that you are having trouble connecting to a loved one or that your current situation (environment, work, relationship, etc.) isn't working for you and you may have to move on to grow.

When it's at the bottom of the cup: You may need to do some spiritual work to reach your full potential right now. Finding happiness in every day.

When it's near the handle: You could be hiding parts of yourself from others. Some self-protection. Like a cocoon.

CAGE

General meaning: Not the most positive thing to see in a reading, a cage represents feeling trapped by someone or something. Feeling unable to escape or feeling stuck in a negative situation.

When it's at the top of the cup: Feeling like you can't communicate your feelings with someone. Hiding your emotions. Honesty and emotional vulnerability are needed.

When it's on the sides of the cup: Staying stuck in a negative situation because you think it will pay off eventually. It won't.

When it's at the bottom of the cup: Someone may be trying to trap you into something. Feeling lost and hopeless in a situation.

When it's near the handle: Marriage of convenience.

CANDLE

General meaning: Candles symbolize enlightenment, peace, and a possible celebration. Whether you are looking for knowledge and shining a light on certain things, finding relaxation, or celebrating life (especially if it looks like a birthday candle), this is a positive symbol to see.

When it's at the top of the cup: People are coming to you for advice.

When it's on the sides of the cup: Needing to finish some chores or tasks.

When it's at the bottom of the cup: Needing peace in your life, dealing with stressful people. Needing to shine a light on a situation in order to understand it and solve it.

When it's near the handle: Burning desire for a love affair.

CLOUD

General meaning: Clouds in your teacup usually represent a lack of clarity on certain issues. Usually manifesting in brain fog, misjudgment, details being muddled, and just a general lack of intuition. You may have trouble making a decision because you don't have all the facts or are not seeing a situation clearly.

When it's at the top of the cup: An important decision is coming up in your life. You'll need to set some kind of goal, so you'll be able to make the right choice for you. Looking for a direction in life.

When it's on the sides of the cup: Trouble defining your goals, feeling a little directionless in life. Difficulty achieving things.

When it's at the bottom of the cup: In order to move forward in life, you need to look into your past and figure out what got you to this point. Suggests that you may be avoiding your past, need clarity, or need healing in order to move on.

When it's near the handle: Confusion. This may not be the best time to trust your judgment as you may not be seeing things clearly.

COIN

General meaning: The first thing that probably comes to mind when you see a coin in your teacup is money—and you're right. Coins represents money, wealth, and financial matters. However, money isn't the only thing coins represent. In tarot, coins, or pentacles, represent the material and physical world, dealing with our health, work, career, environment, and creativity. Associated with the earth element, coins can also represent fertility.

When it's at the top of the cup: Wealth or financial gain is coming into your life. Being able to take control of your finances and being flexible in your private life.

When it's on the sides of the cup: Hard work is paying off with a promotion or raise at your job. Moving up in your career.

When it's at the bottom of the cup: A changing of your environment; you might be moving somewhere, saving money, and keeping your life very private.

When it's near the handle: Very creative time. Making business partnerships, feeling very successful.

Coin size: The larger the coin, the more money you will gain.

CUP

General meaning: A cup, or chalice, represents an offering or sacrifice that will bring a reward in time. What has to be sacrificed can vary, from giving up material goods or decreasing spending to sacrificing relationships. The goal is to gain peace. In tarot, the chalice represents our emotions and is associated with love, feelings, relationships, and the connections we make, and it is ruled by the element of water.

When it's at the top of the cup: You could be moving forward in your spiritual life. This could mean connecting with your higher power, prayer, or getting into the metaphysical through a practice like tarot or crystal healing.

When it's on the sides of the cup: A warning to protect yourself. Some shady people with bad intentions may come into your life. Keep your guard up.

When it's at the bottom of the cup: Here the cup is the representation of your soul. Your spiritual needs may not be met, or you are feeling lost and confused. Find a way back to yourself.

When it's near the handle: You are going on a spiritual journey where your soul may be tried and tested.

DOG

General meaning: Man's best friend, the dog represents loyalty, companionship, and friendliness. When you see a dog in your teacup, it could represent peace, but the placement could indicate how long peace will last and if trouble is coming. Be careful: this dog's bite is much worse than its bark.

When it's at the top of the cup: You're the top dog right now. Everything is working for you; just keep up the good work.

When it's on the sides of the cup: This indicates there are many possibilities in your life right now, whether you go your own way or build a solid community. Remember that dogs are pack animals, so you'll have far more success if you stay with the pack.

When it's at the bottom of the cup: This could spell misfortune as you are at the bottom of the food chain and could be viewed poorly in other people's opinions. It could also mean a breakup, illness, or other misfortune. Bad dog!

When it's near the handle: Someone in your life is very loyal and will stay by your side no matter what.

Dog surrounded by dashes: Estranged friends and jealousy from others.

DONKEY

General meaning: While the first impulse is that the cup is calling you an ass (and that may still be it), it actually means being patient in your life—especially when it comes to money issues. It can also mean working hard in situations.

When it's at the top of the cup: You need to make up your own mind and not just blindly follow the thoughts and beliefs of others.

When it's on the sides of the cup: This is lucky: it means things are going to turn out well in the near future.

When it's at the bottom of the cup: To overcome your problems, you will need hard work and patience.

When it's near the handle: Happy in life.

DOTS

General meaning: Seeing dots is very common in tea readings, mainly because sometimes the leaves just look like dots and not like anything else. It doesn't mean that you had a bad reading or are not imaginative enough. In fact, dots, and their placement, have their own unique meaning.

When it's at the top of the cup: Major financial gains and important recognition from others.

When it's on the sides of the cup: Having a good time, coming into money easily.

When it's at the bottom of the cup: Something big, money-wise, is going to happen, but much later than expected.

When it's near the handle: Business partnerships, getting good financial advice, and letting the good times roll.

A large lump of tea leaves: Extremely lucky!

DRUMS

General meaning: The beating of drums was usually a call to battle, meaning that war and violence were on the way. When you see drums in your teacup, you can expect the same thing: disturbances, conflict, and potential violence. Be careful when you see the drums: trouble is coming.

When it's at the top of the cup: This is the best place to see the drums because it means good news is going to come from other people.

When it's on the sides of the cup: You have a serious problem that is troubling you.

When it's at the bottom of the cup: The fights you have been having will be very public.

When it's near the handle: A lot of fighting with partners and loved ones.

EAGLE

General meaning: One of the most powerful birds in the sky, the eagle is the symbol for authority, power, strength, and dignity.

When it's at the top of the cup: Feeling independent and confident when it comes to making decisions about your life. Feeling sure of yourself and the direction that you are heading in.

When it's on the sides of the cup: You are leading others in an organized manner. Being confident in the decisions you make will be the key to their success.

When it's at the bottom of the cup: You may have power and control issues that can create major conflict.

When it's near the handle: Stay focused and listen.

ELEPHANT

General meaning: Elephants are considered a very lucky animal in most parts of the world and usually bring good things when seen in a tea reading. Elephants represent honor, strength, stability, and patience as well as luck. Could also be a symbol of remembering as "elephants never forget."

When it's at the top of the cup: Good luck is coming your way.

When it's on the sides of the cup: Reliability, dignity, and power.

When it's at the bottom of the cup: Success will come but with some delay.

When it's near the handle: Happiness in life but with great responsibilities as well.

FAIRY

General meaning: I do believe in fairies! Especially the ones found in my teacup. Seeing a fairy in your teacup is often a very good omen meaning that you will be blessed with something magical very soon.

When it's at the top of the cup: Dreams will soon become a reality for you as you have a very important life decision to make. Could also mean freedom when it comes to money.

When it's on the sides of the cup: Time to set goals to achieve your dreams.

When it's at the bottom of the cup: You need to really think about an offer you have been given. Should you take it? Is it worth it?

When it's near the handle: Someone with good intentions is about to enter your life.

FEATHER

General meaning: Despite its lightness in real life, seeing a feather in your cup could bring up some serious and heavy issues. Feathers are often associated with the spiritual and learning a higher truth. They can also represent enchanted awareness and a period of introspection.

When it's at the top of the cup: You are moving on a higher path of spiritual growth.

When it's on the sides of the cup: You need to take things less seriously.

When it's at the bottom of the cup: Overthinking, stressed. You need a break.

When it's near the handle: Needing motivation, feeling like you are not making good choices.

FENCE

General meaning: Fences are made to keep people out and to acknowledge and protect your property, and that's what it represents when you see fences in your reading. You are actively shutting people out of your life or protecting what is yours. It can also be about dealing with obstacles.

When it's at the top of the cup: Swallow your pride and ask for help.

When it's on the sides of the cup: Success in business plans and good health.

When it's at the bottom of the cup: Hidden opportunities will be found in the future.

When it's near the handle: You will have difficulties to overcome.

Broken fence: Finally letting people in.

FISH

General meaning: Hey! What's swimming in my tea? A fish is a lucky omen, sometimes representing fertility, emotion, healing, and cleansing. Seeing many fish in your cup can mean that you have enough energy to overcome any problem. However, be careful: it can also mean a lack of independence.

When it's at the top of the cup: You're ready to adapt to new changes in your life.

When it's on the sides of the cup: It will take some time to adapt to a difficult situation.

When it's at the bottom of the cup: Hard work will finally pay off.

When it's near the handle: Possible minor health issue.

HAMMER

General meaning: The hammer has many meanings: power, strength, virility, and determination; to "lay the hammer down" and show your own power and strength to others. Seeing a hammer means you'll achieve what you want—but you must work very hard for it.

When it's at the top of the cup: Something in your life needs to be fixed.

When it's on the sides of the cup: Get reconnected to the people you have lost touch with.

When it's at the bottom of the cup: You need to focus on the details of what you are doing, or your work will suffer.

When it's near the handle: Hard work is coming your way.

HANDCUFFS

General meaning: Yikes! While seeing a pair of handcuffs anywhere isn't usually a sign of a good time (unless you're into that), seeing them in your teacup does not mean that you're about to hear police sirens anytime soon. Handcuffs represent being held back from success and unable to do what you want, loss of power, and having enemies who are keeping you locked up.

When it's at the top of the cup: A reluctance to move forward in life. Getting stressed out and unable to move forward.

When it's on the sides of the cup: Unable to get the money you need.

When it's at the bottom of the cup: Opportunities for a rebirth in the distant future.

When it's near the handle: Success if you break away from a bad situation.

HAT

General meaning: In life, hats often give us protection from the elements (and a bad hair day), and they represent both protection and concealment in a tea reading as well. Hats can also be personal symbols: if you know someone who is always wearing a certain hat, it could be a reference to them.

When it's at the top of the cup: A false friend.

When it's on the sides of the cup: An opportunity to improve your financial situation.

When it's at the bottom of the cup: A new lover is coming into your life.

When it's near the handle: Develop close allies or people who are willing to help you—trouble is coming.

HEART

General meaning: The heart is one of the universal symbols of love, and seeing a heart in a reading typically means romance, love, and emotions. It represents passion, loyalty, truth, well-being, connection, and love in all of its forms.

When it's at the top of the cup: Love is in your life and you are feeling good!

When it's on the sides of the cup: Romance is going to take center stage in your life very soon.

When it's at the bottom of the cup: A heartbreak of some kind, someone being unfaithful, someone playing games with you. Be careful.

When it's near the handle: A new lover in your life! And they are a keeper!

Lines broken around the heart: A broken heart; getting your heart broken.

Two hearts: Marriage! (Especially if you see a letter next to the hearts, representing a person's initial.)

LAMB

General meaning: The lamb is a popular symbol of spring and innocence; if you see a lamb in your teacup, it is generally a positive symbol meaning that good things are coming into your life, both spiritually and physically. It can also represent an innocent child or timid person in your life.

When it's at the top of the cup: Opportunity for a fresh start, but you must be delicate about the situation.

When it's on the sides of the cup: Successes in business and in health are coming to you in the near future.

When it's at the bottom of the cup: Don't blow your last chance!

When it's near the handle: Coming into contact with a shy person.

Small lamb: A choice you need to make that will create a significant change in your life.

Large lamb: Fear of the unknown.

LEAF

General meaning: While you may see a ton of tea leaves in your cup, if your tea leaves form a leaf image, it's usually a good symbol of luck, health, and prosperity in the future.

When it's at the top of the cup: Happiness in the very near future.

When it's on the sides of the cup: Worries will be over soon.

When it's at the bottom of the cup: Needing to "turn over a new leaf" and move on from the past in order to bring positive changes into your life.

When it's near the handle: Things will get better soon.

LIGHTBULB

General meaning: The universal symbol for "bright idea," a lightbulb usually represents the presence of a bright idea, a solution to a troubling problem, or a spark of inspiration. A new perspective illuminating your mind.

When it's at the top of the cup: Your efforts are not going to waste in this situation. Your bright ideas will be rewarded.

When it's on the sides of the cup: Possible difficulties and setbacks. A creative block. Be alert to things in the shadows.

When it's at the bottom of the cup: Advice to start with a small, simple goal in order to achieve great things in time.

When it's near the handle: A welcome discovery. Something that's been hiding in the shadows of your mind finally comes to light. What you thought was lost is suddenly found!

LIGHTHOUSE

General meaning: Lighthouses guide ships back to shore and, in the same vein, guide us home when we see them in a reading. A lighthouse represents a guiding presence, whether you are following a leader or becoming a leader for others to follow. It can also represent going through an emotional period and standing up for what you believe in. You may be tested, but you must stand tall and shine your light through the darkness and fog.

When it's at the top of the cup: Both nerve and imagination are needed for what you have to do. Talk to someone if you are in a difficult situation that needs to be solved.

When it's on the sides of the cup: A successful business opportunity will greatly improve your personal finances.

When it's at the bottom of the cup: Harmony is needed in your long-term relationships. Your beliefs and morals will be questioned and tested. Someone who is inexperienced may ask you for advice at work.

When it's near the handle: Be careful of fake friends or people who are making your work situation difficult.

MOUSE

General meaning: Eeeek!! A mouse in your teacup! Okay, seeing a symbol of a mouse is not as alarming; it's actually a good sign of recovering from health issues that have been troubling you. But be careful: it could also represent a sneaky person.

When it's at the top of the cup: Independent thinking is needed.

When it's on the sides of the cup: Think twice before acting. You might have to make a budget.

When it's at the bottom of the cup: Slow recovery.

When it's near the handle: Trust your gut, not the "facts."

MUSICAL NOTE

General meaning: Your teacup is singing to you! This is a lovely symbol to see in your cup, especially if you can read music, as it may be suggesting a certain song. But in general, musical notes represent honesty and romance.

When it's at the top of the cup: Peaceful time in love and relationships.

When it's on the sides of the cup: Possibility of a new home.

When it's at the bottom of the cup: Major breakthrough and spiritual revelation.

When it's near the handle: Needing to tell the truth.

OVAL

General meaning: Ovals and open circles are very common in tea readings. They typically represent self-improvement and a return to health.

When it's at the top of the cup: A personal revelation in private.

When it's on the sides of the cup: New business opportunity.

When it's at the bottom of the cup: Good health news coming your way that has been long overdue.

When it's near the handle: Peace at home, family drama ending.

PEAR

General meaning: A pear can be either a lucky or an unlucky symbol, depending on the location. For instance, it could signify money or increased income.

When it's at the top of the cup: If the pear has a bite in it, money is coming your way. If the pear is whole, you may have some delays.

When it's on the sides of the cup: Relief from illness or gaining money illegally.

When it's at the bottom of the cup: Small changes in your life.

When it's near the handle: Someone taking money from you.

Many pears: Receiving money as a gift.

RING

General meaning: When you see a ring, wedding bells are not too far off as it usually represents engagement and/or marriage. It can also represent trust, fidelity, or a conclusion of something—the "happily ever after," if you will.

When it's at the top of the cup: Quick marriage, happening very soon—but it may not last.

When it's on the sides of the cup: A friend giving you a gift.

When it's at the bottom of the cup: Marriage will last a long time.

When it's near the handle: Marriage or marriage proposal coming in the next six months.

Broken ring: Nasty breakup. Heart getting broken.

SPIRAL

General meaning: A spiral in your teacup is a sign of spiritual enlightenment and connecting to the divine. It can also represent a kind of "leveling up" in life, such as a job promotion, becoming wealthy, or just doing some adulting.

When it's at the top of the cup: An opportunity to make your life better—a new challenge, a fresh start, or new ideas that could transform everything.

HERBAL TEA MAGIC *for the* MODERN WITCH

When it's on the sides of the cup: You need to be prepared: a change is coming, but it will be a positive one.

When it's at the bottom of the cup: You need to take control of your own destiny. You have the power to change things; you just have to trust yourself.

When it's near the handle: You need to connect to your spiritual side and/or something higher than yourself. A meeting with destiny.

Multiple spirals: You have many different ideas that could help you be successful. Try to focus and be productive.

STAR

General meaning: When you wish upon a star, or when you see one in your teacup, it represents hope, or wishes that are coming true. Manifestation, dreams, and new possibilities are found in the star. In tarot, the Star card represents hope, faith, and purpose. However, make sure you look at your star carefully. It's important to notice how many lines make up the star. If it's three points, it's good fortune, but if it's four points, it's a warning of sudden danger.

When it's at the top of the cup: Your goals have been met and you are ready to embark on a new journey and adventure. Keep your head up because you will be victorious. Can also signify being seen as a role model in your community.

When it's on the sides of the cup: What you desire is in your grasp; you just need to work extra hard to cross that finish line. Stay organized to achieve things on time.

When it's at the bottom of the cup: You may have to change your goals; the vision that you have for your life isn't obtainable right now. You may also need some help from friends to get organized as your life is a little cluttered.

When it's near the handle: Make a wish! Something you've been dreaming of will finally become true.

Scattered in the teacup: Big winner! You are achieving your dreams and having your wishes granted. A blessing.

SUN

General meaning: Let the sunshine in! When you see the sun in your teacup, it's usually a sign of good times to come. The sun shines its light on the positive things in life and warms you up. This usually represents joy, celebration, playfulness, and new beginnings. This is a warm, happy sign. If you are doing tarot, this could also represent the Sun card for you.

When it's at the top of the cup: All your hard work is about to pay off! Good fortune is smiling on you, and you can rest after working so hard.

When it's on the sides of the cup: You may soon be celebrating some good news, usually having something to do with financial gain.

When it's at the bottom of the cup: You may have trouble finding peace of mind; happiness is feeling out of your reach. You may need some help.

When it's near the handle: Happy days are here! Good vibes only!

SWORD

General meaning: While it could be a little intense seeing a sword in your teacup, the meaning of it is not violent (or anyone challenging you to an actual sword fight). The sword represents power and authority; it is a symbol of strength and courage. In tarot, the suit of swords represents logic, ideas, thought process, ideas, and clarity. It's also associated with the air element. Swords can also represent cutting ties with a person.

When it's at the top of the cup: Your power and authority are being recognized and people are looking up to you. Now is the time to be protective of others and help others.

When it's on the sides of the cup: Someone will be asking for your help and guidance in the near future.

When it's at the bottom of the cup: You're the one who will be needing help from others. Feeling helpless and powerless. Ask for advice from someone older and wiser.

When it's near the handle: Coming up with good, logical ideas will help you come into your personal power. Being "the boss."

TEAPOT

General meaning: Seeing a teapot in a tea reading may suggest that you are drinking too much tea (or spilling it), but it actually represents family matters, especially a parent.

When it's at the top of the cup: Very creative time period.

When it's on the sides of the cup: Money issues could lead to tension at home.

When it's at the bottom of the cup: Reaching a compromise.

When it's near the handle: Call a family member.

UMBRELLA

General meaning: When it rains, it pours, but when you see an umbrella in your teacup, it can suggest that relief is coming, even when you least expect it.

When it's at the top of the cup: Face your problems with confidence—you are protected.

When it's on the sides of the cup: Keep your private life secret for a bit.

When it's at the bottom of the cup: Seek help from a faraway place.

When it's near the handle: Seek help from family.

WAND

General meaning: The wand is associated with magic and the making of magic: manifesting, creation, and making dreams come true. Wands represent creating your own reality, making something out of nothing. In tarot, the suit of wands is associated with energy, spirituality, inspiration, determination, intuition, and creativity. Ambitious and unpredictable, the suit of wands is associated with the fire element.

When it's at the top of the cup: Feeling psychic or meeting with someone who is psychic. Feelings of déjà vu could create problems later.

When it's on the sides of the cup: People may be standing in the way of your success. Ending a relationship in some way.

When it's at the bottom of the cup: A spiritual awakening is coming for you. Your life could completely change.

When it's near the handle: A fresh start, wishes coming true, living your dreams.

WINDMILL

General meaning: Windmills are a good sign when you see them in your teacup, usually representing success after a long period of struggle and hard work. It can also be a symbol of rebirth as a windmill keeps right on moving.

When it's at the top of the cup: Willing to work hard to get the job done. Can represent a practical, down-to-earth person.

When it's on the sides of the cup: People are depending on you for help and guidance. Can also mean moving into a positive situation in the near future. Getting what is fair.

When it's at the bottom of the cup: Life of adventure, travel, and excitement. Feeling free and able to come and go as you please.

When it's near the handle: You will be put in a situation that you will have to work very hard to get out of. Rely on your strength and don't be afraid to ask for help.

RESOURCES

Basile, Lisa Marie. *Light Magic for Dark Times*. Minneapolis: Quarto, 2018.

Cunningham, Scott. *Magical Herbalism: The Secret Craft of the Wise*. Minneapolis: Llewellyn, 1982.

Herstik, Gabriela. *Inner Witch: A Modern Guide to the Ancient Craft*. New York: TarcherPerigee, 2018.

Murphy-Hiscock, Arin. *The Green Witch*. Avon, MA: Adams Media, 2017.

Murphy-Hiscock, Arin. *Spellcrafting: Strengthen the Power of Your Craft by Creating and Casting Your Own Unique Spells*. Avon, MA: Adams Media, 2020.

Murphy-Hiscock, Arin. *The Witch's Book of Self-Care*. Avon, MA: Adams Media, 2018.

Vanderbeck, Paige. *Green Witchcraft: A Practical Guide to Discovering the Magic of Plants, Herbs, Crystals, and Beyond*. Emeryville, CA: Rockridge Press, 2020.

Wigington, Patti. *Herb Magic: An Introduction to Magical Herbalism and Spells*. Emeryville, CA: Rockridge Press, 2020.

ABOUT THE AUTHOR

Elsie Wild is a writer and witch haunting the Adirondack Mountains of Upstate New York. A lifelong student of divination, Wild has been a practitioner of tarot, astrology, numerology, and herbalism for over a decade and has written horoscopes, articles, and guides for various publications. She is the author of *The Secrets of Fortune Telling*, *The Secrets of Spiritual Healing*, *The Little Book of Chakras*, and *The Magic Art of Fortune Telling*, an oracle deck. When she is not writing or casting spells, Wild is arguing with her tarot cards and making terrible puns.